Date Due

APR 16 '69			

THE CIVILIZATION OF THE AMERICAN INDIAN SERIES

[Complete list on pages 144–46]

Early Days among the Cheyenne

and Arapahoe Indians

EARLY DAYS AMONG THE CHEYENNE AND ARAPAHOE INDIANS

John H. Seger

EDITED BY STANLEY VESTAL

UNIVERSITY OF OKLAHOMA PRESS : NORMAN

By the Same Editor

Fandango: Ballads of the Old West (Boston, 1927); ed., *Wah-to-yah and the Taos Trail*, by Lewis H. Garrard (Oklahoma City, 1927); ed., *The Oregon Trail*, by Francis Parkman (Oklahoma City, 1927); *Kit Carson* (Boston, 1928); *Happy Hunting Grounds* (Chicago, 1928); *'Dobe Walls* (Boston, 1929); *Sitting Bull* (Boston, 1932); *Warpath* (Boston, 1933); *New Sources of Indian History* (Norman, 1934); ed., *Early Days Among the Cheyenne and Arapahoe Indians*, by John H. Seger (Norman, 1934, 1956); *The Wine Room Murder* (Boston, 1935); *Mountain Men* (Boston, 1937); *Revolt on the Border* (Boston, 1938); *Professional Writing* (New York, 1938); *The Old Santa Fé Trail* (Boston, 1939); *Writing Magazine Fiction* (New York, 1940); *King of the Fur Traders* (Boston, 1940); *Short Grass Country* (New York, 1941); *Big Foot Wallace* (Boston, 1942); *Writing Non-Fiction* (Boston, 1944); *The Missouri* (New York, 1945); *Jim Bridger* (New York, 1946); *Warpath and Council Fire* (New York, 1948); *Writing: Advice and Devices* (New York, 1950); *Queen of Cowtowns: Dodge City* (New York, 1952); *Joe Meek* (Caldwell, Idaho, 1952); *The Book Lover's Southwest* (Norman, 1955).

First published as a University of Oklahoma Bulletin, March, 1924. Reissued with an Appendix in the Civilization of the American Indian Series, March, 1934. Reset and reissued in new format, March, 1956. Composed and printed by the University of Oklahoma Press, Publishing Division of the University, at Norman, Oklahoma, U.S.A.

FOREWORD

IT IS SELDOM that a book is so readable and in such continuing demand that it is reprinted once more some thirty years after it first appeared. But in this instance it is not surprising for, when first brought out, this book stopped the press; all the compositors put down their sticks to read the copy. Here we have it in new format with type completely reset.

John Homer Seger, the author of these memoirs, was born in Ohio, February 23, 1846, of British and Dutch stock settled in America some time before the American Revolution. His people were pioneers and moved steadily westward as the nation expanded. When he was still a child, his parents removed to Illinois, where they remained until after the Civil War. At the age of seventeen years he enlisted in Company B, Fifty-seventh Illinois Volunteers, and went through the Atlanta Campaign, participating in thirteen engagements. Some time afterward he settled in Kansas, where he lived until employed by the Indian Agent at Darlington, in what is now Oklahoma. A few years later, as narrated below, Seger founded the Indian School and town at Colony, Oklahoma, where he made his home until his death, February 6, 1928.

Probably there was no white man living in his day who had been in such constant and immediate contact with Plains Indians as he.

Some of the interesting material recorded by Seger during his fifty years among the Indians has been lost. But there is quite enough here to convince anyone that the author is thoroughly familiar with the life of early days in western Oklahoma—and that he is a born story-teller who makes the past live for us anew. It is to be regretted that so few historians have his narrative gift.

The material which appears here has been selected for its value in illustrating conditions and characters of early days and is arranged—in the main—chronologically. This method brings out the distinctive merit of these stories—the human side of the Indian, so generally neglected. The "Tradition of the Cheyenne Indians" added in the Appendix in the second edition is from a copy presented to me by Seger himself.

No attempt has been made to do more than arrange the material. Only a very bold man would try to improve on these stories, and an editor would be rash indeed who would tamper with a history, half the interest of which lies in the personality of the teller. Certainly I cannot. I recall too many breathless occasions when, as a boy, I sat up half the night listening to his stories.

John Homer Seger, though a man of limited book-learning, probably knew the Indians with whom he worked during most of his long life better than any literate white man who has left us a record. Here I wish to prefix to his book two stories which he told me but which were not included in his manuscript. I add these because the two incidents explain the beginning of his great influence upon the Indians and his unparalleled understanding of them.

At Darlington, the earliest agency buildings had been made of rough cottonwood logs. These were temporary, and when the Quaker agent decided to erect a new schoolhouse of stone and lumber, he had to employ a stone mason and carpenter, since none of the Quaker employees was qualified. The agent hired John Homer Seger. Soon after, he arrived in Darlington to find the precious lumber neatly stacked near the site of the old schoolhouse, which had just been pulled down. This lumber had been freighted in at great expense by wagon from Wichita, Kansas, 150 miles across the prairie.

That evening, as the agency employees were preparing to eat supper, they saw up-river a great dust cloud lighted by the western sun. The Cheyennes and Arapahoes were coming in from their far-off hunting grounds. All the employees at the agency came out and anxiously watched the approaching horde.

First came the young warriors riding in, painted, plumed, and armed. Then a great ruck of travois, pack animals, and older people, mounted and afoot, their horse herds, dogs, and all.

They swarmed in along the river, close to the buildings. Tipis mushroomed suddenly along the stream. Then the women went looking for firewood with which to cook supper.

The nearest wood was the precious lumber stacked on the prairie convenient to their tents.

Perhaps they thought the Great White Father had provided this fuel for their use; perhaps they did not think. Any-

how, after hiking or riding all day, they were in a hurry to
eat and rest.

When Seger saw these women making off with the precious lumber, he started forward to protest. The Quaker employees tried to stop him, saying, "No, no. Don't interfere. If
you do, they will scalp us all."

But Seger was no Quaker. Though only about five feet,
six inches tall, he was a seasoned veteran of the United States
Army who had seen hard fighting in the Civil War. He could
not endure to see his job going up in smoke without a protest.
Ignoring the words of his pale companions, he hurried out,
took his stand on the pile of lumber and began to talk. He
knew no Indian tongue and had never seen the sign language
used, but he was dreadfully in earnest. And so, as people do
sometimes when talking to foreigners, he began to speak
louder and louder in the vain hope of making his meaning
clear. Before long he was shouting, and supplementing his
words by gestures. When an Indian woman picked up a plank
to carry it off, he would take it away from her and point to
the pile of pickets and logs near by, the remains of the old
schoolhouse. Soon a crowd of Indians gathered, wondering
what all the row was about. But finally one of the chiefs made
out what Seger meant, posted a guard of young warriors about
the lumber and harangued the women, telling them to go else-
where for their fuel.

When Seger was assured that the lumber was safe, he left
it and went into the mess-hall to eat supper. There he found
the Quaker employees pale faced and frightened, thinking
that they had narrowly escaped a massacre.

Next morning, the chiefs came in to pay their respects,

and went first of all to Seger. He, learning through their interpreter what they had come for, took them to the agent. Every day it was the same. They all reported to Seger first, instead of going direct to the agent.

Some years later, when he could talk their language, Seger asked one of the chiefs why they had singled him out in this manner, when he was only a hired man at the agency. The chief laughed and said, "That day you looked so determined and yelled so loud, we thought you must be a big chief from Washington."

By the time the Indians were sufficiently familiar with the white men's ways to understand the nature of Seger's first employment there, he had established his influence and become the superintendent of the school.

The second story I wish to tell explains how Seger quickly gained his uncanny understanding of Indian character and ways of thought. To begin with, of course, he shared many of their qualities: a dauntless courage, a generous heart, a sense of humor, and a frank humanity. But now for the story:

The chiefs had signed a treaty at Medicine Lodge in 1867 and had agreed to put their children to school at the Agency. But Plains Indians lived an intimate family life, men, women, and children together—three, sometimes four generations in one tipi. And their ruling passion was their children. And so all the parents deferred fulfilling their agreement season after season, and only orphans and cripples and sick children were left at the school when the tribe went off to Kansas in spring and fall to hunt buffalo. They were away more than half the year, and could not bear to be separated from their little folks so long.

But to go on these hunts off the reservation it was necessary to have a pass from the agent. One day a chief, accompanied by his small son, rode up on his spotted pony and dismounted at the agency. The chief had dressed his boy handsomely in beaded buckskins, sleek otter-skin wraps for his two braids, bone breastplate, and feather fan. His face was painted with vermilion, like the part in his gleaming black hair. The chief went into the office and asked Seger for a pass to hunt buffalo.

Seger answered, "Give me your son."

The Chief protested, "Why should I give you my son?"

Seger replied, "So that I can make a white man of him."

The chief laughed at this absurdity. He had heard that song before. Said he, "Then give me a white boy to make an Indian of."

As the chief had expected, Seger replied, "I have no white boy to give you." Then, to the chief's surprise, Seger added, "But if you will give me your son to put to school this winter, I will come to your camp next summer and you can make an Indian of me."

The humor of this proposal caught the chief's fancy. Besides, he wanted that pass, and had been caught in his own trap. He agreed to leave the boy with Seger.

But next summer, sure enough, here came the chief to pick up the white man and carry him off to his camp. Seger went cheerfully along, for he saw that he could do himself and the agency much good on this novel expedition.

When they arrived at the tribal encampment, where hundreds of tipis stood in a great circle, the chief rode around shouting in a crier's far-carrying voice, "I have brought this white man to camp to make an Indian of him. Every Indian in the camp must help."

Most of that summer Seger remained in that camp, wearing Indian clothes, learning Indian manners, and observing Indian life. Every time he turned around, someone would remark, "That is not the Indian way to do it. An Indian does it this way."

It seemed that nearly everything he did was wrong. "Don't turn your toes out; walk straight. Toe in."

Seger demanded, "Why?"

His mentor then explained, "Because an Indian trail is narrow. If you turn out your toes, you will trip over the grass and underbrush."

Men, women, and children all joined in the game, lessoning their genial visitor, and every time they corrected him he asked the same question, "Why?"

By the end of that summer he had had a course conducted by several thousand Indians in their ways of thought and motives, in Indian customs and the reasons therefor. No other white man ever had such thorough schooling in those subjects. No wonder he understood Indians so remarkably well.

W. S. CAMPBELL (*Stanley Vestal*)

Norman, Oklahoma
December 30, 1955

CONTENTS

ILLUSTRATIONS

Early Days among the Cheyenne

and Arapahoe Indians

Courtesy Muriel H. Wright

JOHN   H.   SEGER

Courtesy Oklahoma Historical Society

BRINTON   DARLINGTON

Chapter I

I GO TO THE

INDIAN COUNTRY

SOON AFTER President Grant inaugurated his Quaker "peace policy" among the Indians, an agency was established for the Southern Cheyennes and Arapahoes, on the bank of the Canadian River where Darlington, Oklahoma now stands. Brinton Darlington was appointed agent. He was a staunch Quaker and fully in sympathy with the belief that the government could best civilize the Indian by bringing him in contact with Christian people. He also believed that by confining him to a reservation lawless whites could be excluded. The Indian children were to be educated and aided to give their parents instruction in farming and in stock-raising.

Major Weinkoop, the military agent, gladly turned the commissary over to Agent Darlington, who began at once to lay out the grounds of his house and office on the spot where Darlington is now located. Quaker employees came in from Iowa, Indiana and other states. But it was soon found that it was one thing to develop a theory of how to civilize the In-

---

3

dian and quite another thing to put it into execution. There were many houses to build, beef to herd and issue, supplies for the Indians to be received and given out, as well as farming ground to be broken out and fenced. A sawmill had to be constructed and logs cut and hauled to make the necessary lumber and all this work had to be done with a few hands.

The first houses were rough cottonwood and picket houses consisting of from one to three or four rooms. This lumber was green and soon shrank very badly, leaving the houses open and very cold to live in, and the zealots cooled in their desire to aid the red man. There were many changes in the force.

Each spring Agent Darlington sent his employees out to instruct and assist some Indians in farming. A few children had been put to school, but the majority of those of school age accompanied their parents when on the buffalo hunt, which was nearly two-thirds of the time. The Indians very naturally preferred hunting buffalo to farming. Only when game was scarce did they come to the agency and draw rations and they seemed to be satisfied with the conditions as they were.

In 1872 Brinton Darlington died, leaving conditions with the Indians very much as I have described them above. Some may think this a very poor showing for three years of hard work, but few will ever know the real good that was done. The Indians had learned to love and respect at least one white man. They had learned that all white men were not whiskey peddlers and horse thieves. In Brinton Darlington they discovered a white man whom they could both love and respect. At his funeral many stern warriors shed tears, and they have ever since cherished and revered his memory. To this day the sign for agent is the motion of taking something from the mouth—which sprung from Darlington's jocose trick of taking out his false teeth to surprise them.

Few persons reap the reward and credit they deserve for work of this kind—but I know that much of what has since been accomplished in the civilization of the Cheyenne and Arapahoe Indians is owing to the work of Brinton Darlington.

After Darlington's death John D. Miles, agent for the Kickapoos in Kansas, was transferred to the Cheyenne and Arapahoe agency to take charge. Miles was in the prime of life and of good business ability. He took hold of the work of civilizing the Indian with energy and zeal. He was accompanied by his amiable wife, a woman of marked ability and judgment. "Aunt Lucy" all the people at the agency soon called her. She was a great help and support to her husband and a sympathetic advisor and friend to every employee.

Agent Miles was also a Quaker, but the Quaker employees had somewhat thinned out. The incommodious buildings and isolated life more than any feeling of alarm caused them to turn their faces toward civilization. Their idea of establishing a friendly and brotherly feeling between the white man and the Indian had succeeded, but the practical results had not fulfilled their expectations. One Quaker in his parting talk to the Indians with whom he had labored for five years said, "I have been trying to get thee to follow the white man's road and thee has followed it until thee got to the white man's table and there thee have stopped. And I believe some great calamity must befall thee before thee will be willing to go further."

5

The red people soon understood that the unbounded kindness of the Quakers was to win them to follow the white man's ways, and they met the white man halfway. They always greeted him with a warm handshake and sometimes went so far as to rub noses, a manner of greeting that the white brother did not encourage and which is now obsolete—but when it came to the point of giving up his hunting, the Indian had many good reasons to offer why he should not do so. He said, "I do not know how to farm, but I do know how to hunt. I like hunting better. It is our custom to hunt. Moreover, while I am learning to farm, my family will starve. There are plenty of buffalo and they are the natural food of my people. They belong to us, and why should we not hunt them? The white men like the buffalo robes and send men from the rising sun to buy them. Why should we not kill the buffalo and dress the robes and sell them to the white men?"

After three years of instructing and coaxing, the Quakers had begun to understand the task that was before them. They saw that the best results would be obtained by getting the children into school and instructing them there. There had been an attempt made to carry on a day school by Mr. and Mrs. Townsend in January, 1871. In April Alfred J. Standing (who afterwards continued a faithful and active worker in Indian schools and for many years was Assistant Superintendent of the large Indian school in Pennsylvania) took charge and Miss Julia Cathel was his co-worker. Mr. Standing taught the Cheyennes and Miss Cathel the Arapahoes. The schoolhouse was an unpainted cottonwood shack, and the furniture consisted of a couple of tables and a few benches with no blackboard. In order to separate the Cheyenne and Arapahoe

children from each other Mr. Standing moved his school into
a picket building with a dirt roof and floor. This might be
called "the ground floor of Indian school-work." In this building the Indian children were taught what a school was, a
thing they did not know before. One of the first difficulties
which had to be met was getting the children to come at the
right hour. They were not used either to going to bed or
getting up at any specified time, and as they had no time-
pieces, punctuality was out of the question, so Mr. Standing
summoned them by going through the camp blowing a cow's
horn.

This school lasted through April, May and a part of June.
The Indians then went out on their summer buffalo hunt for
the purpose of getting buffalo skins to make lodge cloth of.
Every Indian left the agency taking all the children with them
and not a single pupil called for his diploma before leaving.

At times Mr. Standing went out to the camps with pictures
and books and taught wherever he could collect a class. In
this way he got acquainted with the children and cultivated
the friendship of the parents. The Indians invited him to go
with them on their hunt and to continue his teaching. While
a flying battery might have been an appropriate thing to
send along with them, the agent did not think it best to intro-
duce a portable schoolhouse into service, so Mr. Standing
did not go.

The Arapahoe mission, as it was called, was then built.
It was commodious enough to take in thirty-five children and
to board them and lodge them. This building was ready for use
when John D. Miles took charge.

The new agent employed Joshua Trueblood and his wife

Matilda for teachers and a widowed sister, Mrs. Martha Hudgins, was installed as matron. They were all Quakers and competent people for the work. Many of the first Quaker employees who had entered the service had returned to their homes, and the agent and his family, Joshua Trueblood, his wife and head farmer, Joseph Hoag, were the only Quaker employees left. The rest of the force did not even pretend that they were in the service through a missionary spirit nor solely for the good of the Indian.

Agent Miles grasped the situation. It was necessary to provide better quarters for the employees and as the appropriation with which to do it was small, he placed more dependence upon whether his employees knew how to do the work and were willing to do it, than upon the religious denomination to which each man belonged. It was more important that the men who took care of the cattle to be issued to the Indians, understood how to handle long-horned Texas steers than that they believed in any church or special creed. Thus Tom George, a rushing and skillful carpenter of Maskota, Kansas, was brought to the agency as government carpenter. Tom did not belong to any church, but like Doctor McClure of "the Bonnie Brier Bush" he did not swear except when strictly necessary.

William Darlington, son of the former agent, was engineer and could not only run the sawmill engine, but was able to repair any part of it when it was out of order.

Agent Miles thought he needed one more man to do mason work, as there would be plastering to do, walls to lay, chimneys to build and lime to burn. His appropriation would not admit of the hiring of a man for each of these things; he needed a man who could do all these different kinds of mason work, a kind of Jack-of-all-trades, who would be willing and capable of doing any kind of work that needed to be done and for which provision had not been made. On inquiring for such a man he was told by Joshua Trueblood that there was such a man as he needed at New Malden, Atchison County, Kansas, by the name of John H. Seger. The agent, having business up in that part of the country at that time, came to see me and engaged me to work at the agency for one year at six hundred dollars per annum. I was to be on hand by January first. It was in this way that I came in contact with the Indians. I was at that time an active young fellow of twenty-nine years of age with not much capital beyond good muscles and sound health.

Chapter II

THE INDIANS NAME ME
"JOHNNY SMOKER"

THE INDIANS were nearly all away on their winter hunt when I arrived at Darlington on Christmas day, and the whole agency force was employed in this work of tearing down its old buildings and rebuilding in more substantial form. I had been hired to do mason work, but as the cold weather made it impossible I reported to Agent Miles and was instructed to report to the farmer who was in charge of the working force. The farmer asked me if I knew how to chop down trees and saw logs. I told him I had been employed in the Wisconsin Pinery one winter and had learned to swing an axe. He asked me if I had any objections to going eight miles down the North Fork to camp while cutting the logs. I told him I had not.

Next day I packed up my blankets and bedding and went into camp, where I remained with one other employee five weeks, living in a tent and cutting logs, during which time the weather was very cold for this climate. Snow was on the ground most of the time.

Finally the weather became warm and spring-like and I was instructed to report back to the agency again where I began the work of laying a foundation for an office for the agency doctor.

After my five weeks' hermitage, eight miles away, the society of the people at the agency was very pleasant, though the only amusement or recreation which the young people enjoyed was song service or prayer-meeting. Musical instruments were very scarce.

When spring came and the grass grew green, the Indians began to return to the agency from their winter's hunt. To those of us who had not been acquainted with them, everything about these camps was novel and interesting. As they came streaming in and went to work setting up their camps near the agency I studied their manners, looks and customs very closely, and I went among them freely. It seemed as though every Indian I met were a chief and expected some special recognition on that account, but I soon discovered that there were chiefs and chiefs, and that only a few were entitled to that honor. These among the Arapahoes were Left Hand, Yellow Bear, Little Raven, and Bird Chief, while Big Mouth, Cut Finger, Yellow Horse, White Crow, and a few others were but minor chiefs or band men.

The leaders of the Cheyennes at that time were Bull Bear, Little Robe, Red Moon, Stone Calf and White Horse; Old Whirl Wind, Old Big Jake, Black Kettle and White Shield were subordinates.

The Arapahoes were friendly, but the Cheyennes were proud and less inclined to fraternize with the whites. They were a stronger, more warlike people. They had fought their way for a thousand miles to this country and were not disposed to bow the neck.

Soon after I entered the service I was in a Cheyenne camp where they had just finished dressing a boy six years old in the full costume of a warrior. His scalp lock was braided, his hair parted in the middle with a red streak drawn along the parting, his buckskin leggings were fringed at the side, his moccasins were artistically beaded and had long fringes of buckskin at the heels, his bow with sinew string was tightly strung, his quiver of arrows was well feathered and steel-pointed, his face was painted with care and taste. I never saw a more completely equipped warrior than was represented in the dress and arms of this Indian boy.

I saw that some special significance lay in it, and watched him with interest after his grandfather and uncles and aunts had all in turn criticised or put a finishing touch to his make-up. At last he was pronounced perfect. Straightening up proudly, he said, "I am now going out to kill a white man." The involuntary laugh of all his friends and their looks of approval, showed me that he had uttered the proper thing. It was at that moment I realized that the only way to civilize the red man was through his children; so long as they regarded the white man as their natural enemy, nothing could be done.

I soon discovered that the best type of Indians did not stay round the agency. As a rule, those who had the least force and ambition lolled about, keeping up the brotherly-love carried on by Miles and his teachers. Yellow Horse, White Crow, Cut Finger, Big Mouth, and a few others of the Arapahoes lolly-gagged around the agency a good deal of the time calling on the Quaker employees. They made visits at meal time, generally, and showed cordial appreciation of their white sister's cooking. Sometimes the Quaker housewife would fry eggs for them (which they enjoyed greatly), and while they ate recommended them to settle down and raise their own chickens when they could have eggs in abundance.

They agreed with this plan and once Yellow Horse said if he only had a squaw hen and some eggs he would give his undivided attention to the raising of poultry. So a setting of eggs and a hen that was ready to set were furnished him. He located the hen at the head of his bed where he could study the mysteries of raising poultry with the least trouble to himself.

Just as the hen had gotten down to business Yellow Horse received notice that he must pack his camp and go out on the buffalo hunt with a party that was to be sent out to procure meat for the camp at the agency. A runner had been sent in notifying them that buffalo was plenty a short distance from the agency. In vain Yellow Horse explained how ruinous it would be to his poultry project to move his hen before she had hatched her brood. Yellow Horse was well posted in all the details of setting a hen as he had called on some white families at meal time two or three times each day since he had embarked in the poultry business to get instructions in hen-setting. But the band he belonged to could not understand the situation and Yellow Horse could not change the edict.

Finally a council was called in which it was decided that Yellow Horse might remain provided he would put up a feast to the band he belonged to. Yellow Horse was very much pleased at this decision and to carry it into effect caught up his best buffalo horse and sold it for thirty dollars and spent all the money in providing the feast. Thus the first crisis in his new industry was met.

A few hogs had been given to them in the hope that they would care for them. But when the word came for them to go on the buffalo hunt they had no place to keep them. They got permission to put their pigs in the agent's pen, but when they returned from the buffalo hunt a few months later they took their porkers out and killed them to make a feast, so that in one day the hog industry vanished. They were always ready to have another hog given to them and quite willing that the giver should raise and fatten it for them.

Black Kettle was given a hog which he took home and kept till it became very tame and gentle. The small children could ride it, and it was accustomed to enter the lodge and lie by the fire in cold weather. In the spring when the agency people began to make gardens this hog became very troublesome. Black Kettle was notified to take care of it, but gave no heed to the notice. Finally it was caught and corralled. Soon after, Black Kettle missed his hog from the family circle and began at once to inquire for it. He learned that it had been shut up. Going to the agent he asked, "Why has my hog been put in the guard house? I am sure he has not done anything wrong intentionally."

The agent told him that the hog rooted up the potatoes that the white people planted.

Black Kettle replied, "The hog meant no harm by that. It is a hog's nature to root. He likes potatoes and eats them because he is hungry. The fault is not with the hog but with the persons who scattered the potatoes over the ground knowing that the hog would root after them. In camp we put the things we don't want the hog to eat in the forks of a tree or hang them on a pole out of the reach of the hog." All of which, spoken seriously, shows how primitive they were in the business of raising poultry and pork. Hunting buffalo was an industry—raising potatoes was an illogical sort of amusement, and as buffalo were plenty why worry over the white man's ways of living?

Everything we did was as interesting to them as their customs and ways were to us. Especially did they like to watch the white women as they went about their daily duties. To do this they often thronged the windows and pressed their faces against the panes, scrutinizing every movement of the family inside the house. They very naturally inferred that the window was intended to be used as much for looking into the house as for giving light and for looking out—a point of view the whites did not appreciate.

When the family meals were served the scenes inside became still more interesting to the red brother, and generally some of the chiefs or head men would calmly enter and sit down to eat with the family. The Quaker employees fed them as long as the food held out, for they were attempting to win their friendship and acquaintance. At first when the visitors were few the plan worked first rate, but when one or two thousand were camped about, even the most zealous Quakers were obliged to set a limit to their hospitality.

How to prevent the Indians from crowding into their homes and filling all the available chairs at the table without giving offense, was a difficult problem, for all the warriors carried their weapons wherever they went, and each Indian woman wore a savage-looking butcher-knife in her belt, while the few Quaker families were unarmed and helpless. It soon became necessary to lock the outside doors to keep the friendly Arapahoes from entering and taking complete possession of the houses. As they were always hospitable, sharing their food and their lodge, they did not hesitate to feast with their Quaker friends. The white people in their opinion had unlimited stores of food—and this food was very tasty after some months of buffalo meat.

As spring came on Agent Miles began talking to them again about farming and living in houses. A delegation of chiefs had been to Washington the previous autumn and had talked long with the officials there in regard to their future. Among other things the chiefs had promised to put their children into the boarding school, and to make a start in learning to farm, but it was one thing for the chiefs to promise and another thing for the young men to follow the plow.

Very little headway was made during this spring in getting them interested in the soil, but Big Mouth offered to accept a house if the government would build it for him, so even before all the employees were comfortably quartered a house was put up for him. It was a story-and-a-half frame building made from native lumber, with two rooms on the first floor and two on the second. A large stone fireplace was constructed at the end of the building and the house was plastered, and taking it all together it was the most comfortable residence at the agency, excepting the agent's house and the boarding school building.

The agent had made every effort to complete this building

before Big Mouth came in from the buffalo hunt, but owing to the inclement weather, the work was delayed, and Big Mouth arrived with twenty lodges of his people soon after the house was enclosed. He put up his camp near the house and seemed very anxious to have it finished, as he wished to show that he had not forgotten his promise to the Great Father.

When I got ready to plaster the house, one of the older employees said: "You'll have a whole lot of trouble at that work. The Indians will be there in crowds, and the young men and boys will scratch up the walls. You'll never get them smooth. Why, when the agent's house was plastered he had to sit on the porch all through the work to keep the boys from defacing the walls before they were dry. He was the only man the Indians would pay any attention to. Sometimes he had to take hold of them and push them out and away from the building before they would let the work alone. No other employee could do this, but they respected his gray hairs, and would not resist him. They'll make it lively for you!"

With this forewarning I began to plan to prevent the boys from destroying my work. It happened that the man who mixed the mortar for me had lost two of his front teeth, and wore some artificial ones fastened upon a plate. He had a trick of taking this plate with the two teeth on the end of his tongue and running it out of his mouth. It seemed that he had two teeth on the end of his tongue, and I concluded to try the experiment of having him pose as a "medicine man," or conjurer, for I had learned in what awe the red children held those wise men. So when we began plastering this house, I said: "Joe, whenever you see a boy about to deface the walls, run up to him and motion him to get away and at the same time run out your tongue at him—that'll fix him." Neither of us could speak a word of Indian or communicate in any way with them.

Soon after we began working a party of young men came trotting into the room. "Now's your chance, Joe," I shouted.

Facing them and pointing to the door he ordered them out, and when they did start, ran out his fanged tongue. Instantly they rushed for the door, apparently in great fright, falling over one another in their effort to escape. They ran all the way to camp and reported what they had seen, I suppose, for immediately a large party of young people, both men and women, came hurrying towards our building. They did not come up very close, but eyed Moreland closely, seeking some indication of his supernatural powers. They were careful not to get very near and fled like antelope when he approached them. They finally made signs asking him to run out his tongue again. Evidently some of the newcomers began to doubt the truth of the report, so to satisfy them he again stuck out his tongue; whereupon they all uttered cries of surprise or fear and scampered off to camp.

We were troubled no more during the day, but when we went to our dinner I foresaw that they might take advantage of our absence and scrape the mortar from the walls, so I locked the doors, but raised the window as I was anxious to have the plaster dry as fast as possible. I ate my dinner hurriedly, and returned to the building.

Before I got there I heard a peculiar noise in the house, and knew that a lot of half-grown boys were at work on the walls. When I reached the door I found them all in the second

18

Mr. Seger supervising Indians at work at Colony.

story where the mortar was fresh and furnished a better field for their hieroglyphics.

The work before me was to get them out of the house, and as I could not talk to them I saw I must resort to some other means of hastening their exit, so I jumped in at the window and began hopping up and down on the floor and screaming at the top of my voice. I threw my arms around in wild gestures and flung my hat on the floor. They came running down at once and when they saw me apparently in crazy convulsions they tumbled out the window in a heap and fled to camp, scarcely daring to look back. They troubled me no more while I worked on this building.

At last my work was completed and Big Mouth was notified that his house was ready for his occupation and the keys were delivered to him. After looking it all over he said very gravely to the agent: "The white man's tepee is altogether too small for my family. I have seven wives and each of them has several children. I can't possibly move into this house. Instead of four rooms I should have, at least, seven rooms. Unless each wife has a room for herself, she will be angry and mar my peace and quietude." He saw the agent's disappointment, and added: "I'll tell you what I will do, Father. I will move my camp close to the house and use it for my dogs to sleep in and I will store my raw buffalo hides there, while my seven wives are engaged in tanning them." And this is how he used his new house.

When Little Raven was talked to on the subject of dwelling in a cabin he said: "I promised the Great Father that I would start on the white man's road and that I would live in a wooden tepee if the government would build it for me, but

I am principal chief and the government should not build anything for me poorer than the house the Great Father lives in. I do not care to live in a little log tepee."

The agent told him that the government could not build such houses for all of them, because they had not the money to use for that purpose.

Little Raven replied: "I do not think that is the true reason, for when I was in Washington I saw the government making money. I think that all the Great Father needs to do when he has not enough is to hire more men and make more. There are plenty of poor white men in Washington who would like to work for the government making money."

The agent could not very well explain to him how money received its value, and the discussion rested at that point.

As the camp surrounding the agency finally numbered nearly one hundred lodges it formed a most interesting sight, especially at night when every tepee was lighted by an inside fire, a rosy glow which outlined the shape of each lodge on the darkness. It was a pleasant and sociable life. In passing through camp at night one heard on every side the hum of cheerful voices. Some were singing low songs, some were talking to old men, relating stories of their adventurous lives, while here and there a young man and woman might be seen standing beneath the shelter of a single blanket, whispering love messages to each other. Children played in groups, dogs barked and whined. The whole camp was filled with life and merriment, till midnight.

At last the children became too tired to play and curled down in the lodges, sometimes all in a heap, and wandered away into the silence of dreamland. The old women covered the fires and went to bed, and by midnight quiet reigned, except when some restless dog sent up a yell, to be joined by others in a wild chorus, winding up with the far-off coyote echo. Then every one slept profoundly and comfortably.

In the morning the camp awoke in very much the same order in which it retired. The men who had charge of the horses rose at early dawn and went forth upon the plain, ropes in hand, solitary and silent. The others awoke only when sleep no longer satisfied them. Duties were not pressing and breakfast was simple. When they had eaten and had sauntered over to the agency, the employees, who had long since had their coffee, would be engaged in their routine duties and these duties amused the red people all day—till the time for their second meal came around.

During their stay at the agency the red men spent much time walking around examining the strange tools the white people used, noting their peculiarities of dress and gesture; but some of the Indian women were very industrious, and employed their time tanning robes, which they traded at the store in exchange for gay-colored blankets and shawls and calicos for dresses. The men bought strouding blankets, which were afterwards ornamented with beadwork by women and these they wore in place of the old-time whitened summer robes.

The agency employees were frequently surrounded by a crowd of these children of the Plains while engaged in special work. How to convince the Indian that he ought to throw off the blanket (which he wore with such grace) and to put on the white man's overalls, instead of standing around and looking at the white man work and sweat and tug all day long—

that was the problem. The red man saw no necessity for this change and consulting his own wishes decided that work was a white man's penalty—an evil to be avoided. The white man earned his living that way because he was a poor hunter!

The agent placed his greatest hopes on the boarding school which he called "the entering wedge of civilization." If new wants could be created which the red man could not supply by the chase then he would listen to advice.

While the chiefs who had visited Washington, as before mentioned, had promised the Great Father that they would put their children in school, they did so only to the point of gathering up a few, stupid, scrofulous orphans. "These you may have," they said. As the boys objected to having their braids of hair cut, they were allowed to keep them, and as they could not speak any English, a few months' instruction made very little change in them. The school was looked at by the young men and those who took a pride in their tribe and who thought the Indian superior to the white man as a menace to their tribal life. The pupils were taunted by other children who called: "See the white man! See the white girl!" as they passed, and this did not make education popular.

The children went to school in the morning but when they were let out to play quite generally scampered away to camp, and when they had thrown off their uniforms could not be identified by the teachers. It was a very difficult matter to keep anything like a fair attendance by any means at hand.

I used to pay frequent visits to the schools, to visit Joshua Trueblood the superintendent, and each time I could not help but note how little progress had been made. He had very little control over them.

On one occasion while visiting at the school I found him in the playroom with his wards all around him waiting for their retiring hour. The outside doors were locked to keep them from running away to camp, and part of them were drumming on tin cans, on the stove lids, or anything that would vibrate or make a sound; while others were singing native songs at the top of their voices.

Mr. Trueblood was standing in the midst of them, wearing a bland Quaker smile, which seemed to be all he could do to let them know that he was friendly to them and wished them well.

As the noise was so great that he would not converse, I began to reason upon the situation. "Why don't Trueblood lead them in some play or song, which would prove interesting to them?" I queried. Acting upon this thought, I stepped out into the middle of the floor and when a boy looked up at me I made a queer face at him; he laughed and called attention to me and cried out: "Do it again."

I again made up a worse face and others began to laugh, and soon the entire crowd gave me their undivided attention. Up to this moment I had not uttered a word, but as they fell silent I began to sing a little school song I had learned when a boy, a "round" called "Johnny Smoker"—the words were accompanied with gestures of how Johnny Smoker blew his horn, beat his drum and triangle, and played his violin and cymbal. It ended up by showing how he smoked his pipe.

Before the song was ended the children rose of their own

accord and formed a ring around me and when the song came to an end they cried out in chorus, "Do it again." I repeated the song several times, and soon they were imitating the gestures and trying to repeat the words after me.

When it was time for them to retire, Mr. Trueblood expressed astonishment that I had succeeded in quieting the uproar and getting the children really to take an interest in anything that a white man would do.

After this whenever I went to the school the children would gather around me and cry out, "Johnny Smoker," wishing me to sing for them again. They soon learned to sing the song themselves and it was not unusual to hear them either in camp or on the school grounds, singing "Johnny Smoker" together with all the gestures and variations. In a short time I became known to all the Indians as "Johnny Smoker," and for some fifteen years after the name hung to me, applied not only by the Indians, but by the agency employees as well.

One day while I was busy laying stone for the foundation of a building a group of the schoolboys came up and wanted me to stop work and sing "Johnny Smoker" to them. As well as I could, I made them understand that I had to work and could not stop to sing, whereupon one of the boys went to helping me. He began by bringing me stones, and I was surprised at his good judgment in picking out the right stone, and he soon seemed to know just how it ought to be laid. I encouraged him in all this, letting him take my stone hammer and giving him some instructions. He became very much interested in his work, so much so that when the school bell rang for supper he heard it not, but kept on at work.

Finally when I quit work for the day I realized that the

boy by remaining at work had missed his supper, so I went to the school with him and explained to Mr. Trueblood that the boy was not a truant, but had been so busy helping me that he did not notice the bell, and asked that the boy might have his supper. Mr. Trueblood said, "What? Have you succeeded in getting Wauconich to do any work? I have never been able to get him to do so much as carry in an armful of wood."

The springtime passed by, and almost no progress was made in getting the Indians to farm, and when they went out for their summer hunt their children were as usual taken out of school. Only some fifteen or twenty remained, and life at the agency became very monotonous.

I missed my red friends very much. There was very little news from the outside world. The only excitement came with the news that some party of desperadoes was passing through the agency or lurking near, men who had committed some depredation along the frontier and had taken refuge in the Indian Territory. There were many such in those days. On several occasions the agency forces hesitantly mounted the available horses at the agency and went out to endeavor to capture some of these desperadoes—to no purpose, however.

Chapter III

THE CHEYENNES
GROW RESTLESS

THE TERRITORY swarmed with hired buffalo hunters whom
the Indians cordially hated—for they were destroying the
game in thousands. Agent Miles soon saw that something
must be done to protect his wards from these and from whiskey peddlers, or a war with the Cheyennes would surely arise.
To this end he procured the appointment of two United States
Deputy Marshals, who were to accompany the Indians on
their hunts and arrest any man found violating the law in regard to selling liquor to red men. Miles himself, and Joseph
Hoag, who was the agency farmer, also went out to the hunting grounds, determined to do everything in their power to
avoid an outbreak.

Miles found many men from Kansas, (some with their families), who had moved out on the buffalo range to hunt and
to kill meat for their own use. A long drought had left the
new settlers almost destitute, and to kill buffalo seemed to
them the only way to bridge over the winter and provide food
for their families.

Agent Miles with his marshal and a detail of soldiers, which he procured from Camp Supply, drove these people from the buffalo range and brought many of them to Darlington, where they were started for Kansas to their homes.

The newspapers in western Kansas denounced Agent Miles in their columns most vehemently for this action, even suggesting that if he came through that country they would hang him. They did not understand that this was done to prevent the Indians from going on the warpath and killing, perhaps, the very families that were trying to subsist in this way.

With the help of his marshals Miles also succeeded in arresting several peddlers in the act of selling whiskey. All kegs were split open and the liquor poured on the ground, and those connected with its sale were taken to Topeka under arrest. The United States court was in session at the time and the prisoners were tried and promptly convicted and sentenced to prison.

The main witnesses in this case were blanket Indians who could not speak a word of English, and an effort was made, on the part of the defense, to break down their testimony. To make sure that they were not posted in regard to what evidence had been given and to prevent an understanding with the interpreter, they were brought into the court-room one at a time, and after their testimony had been given they were sent out through another door. In this way no witness had any knowledge of what the person preceding him had said. While old Spotted Wolf, who was one of the witnesses, was in one of the vestibules adjoining the court-room, waiting his turn, the deputy marshal in charge of him saw him retire to one corner of the vestibule, and after taking certain attitudes of worship to the spirits, he was seen to repeat something in Indian.

The deputy marshal, excited and suspicious, inquired of the interpreter, "What is the old scoundrel saying?"

The interpreter replied: "Spotted Wolf is praying to the Great Spirit to help him tell the truth, and to guard him from anything that would appear to be a falsehood."

This made a deep impression upon the marshal, convincing him that Spotted Wolf intended to tell the truth as he saw it, and going before the court under oath he testified to what he had seen Spotted Wolf do and his words went far toward convincing the court and jury that the old Cheyenne understood the nature of an oath and was competent to give evidence. The whiskey peddlers were punished.

This trip of Spotted Wolf and the Indians to Topeka, the capital of Kansas, was a wonderful experience to them, as they at that time had seen very little of white people's ways of living, except at the agency and at some frontier posts and trading points. Agent Miles wishing them to be pleased with their trip, so that thereafter it would not be difficult to get others to go on similar errands, had given $10.00 to Spotted Wolf, the most prominent man in the party, to be used in any way he wished while on his trip. He had said: "You will see many fine things while at the stores in the city, and you will probably like to have some of them." After reaching Topeka Spotted Wolf and wife sallied out into the business part of town to spend their $10.00. They looked in the show windows as they passed along, and finally their attention was attracted to a very handsome lady's hat in the window of a millinery

store. It carried a large ostrich feather, and was gay with
bright ribbons. Spotted Wolf and his wife, after gazing at it
and talking earnestly, entered the millinery store and asked
the price of the hat.

The milliner displayed the hat to them and showed them
how it should be worn and said the price (to them) was
just $10.00.

They at once turned over the money and possessed themselves of the hat. Mrs. Spotted Wolf put it on her head and
they at once started back to their boarding place. Usually Indian women follow the men when walking, but in this case
Spotted Wolf insisted that his wife should go ahead that he
might better admire the hat. He thought it would undoubted-
ly create a sensation as she passed (as it did), for Mrs. Spotted
Wolf was one of the worst-looking old women I ever saw and
with her Indian dress and blanket in contrast with the $10.00
hat presented a ludicrous appearance—but of this the proud
and generous husband was happily unaware.

As spring came on, the Indians returned very bitter and
sullen. Many of their ponies had been stolen, the whiskey
men had got the better part of their winter's hunt, and Chief
Little Robes' son was suffering from a broken knee. It could
easily be seen, by those acquainted with the Indians, that they
were in warlike mood. They began to fear the destruction of
the buffalo and resented the increasing swarm of white hunters. One day a party of Arapahoes came marching into the
agency and we soon learned that they had come to attend
a scalp dance.

While the idea was shocking to most of us, we were all
curious to see the dance. When I reached the place of the

dance I saw a large party of Arapahoes, both women and men, gathered in an open space in the midst of the agency. All were painted and the men were armed, and one old woman with her face painted black was carrying a bloody scalp on the end of a pole. She sang and sobbed by turns, as she marched ahead of the procession. When they reached the place appointed for the dance, they all formed in a circle with the old woman in the center holding high the bloody scalp. I was told that the scalp had been taken from the head of a Pawnee Indian. The Pawnees some years back had killed an Arapahoe, and some friends of the murdered man having met a Pawnee while out on a buffalo hunt had killed him in retaliation and took his scalp. The old woman who was carrying the scalp was the mother of the Arapahoe who had been slain. They all began to dance around the scalp, sometimes weeping and sometimes singing, while the old woman occasionally lowered the trophy for the admiration of the bystanders. When she passed me she held the scalp within a few inches of my face, and asked in Indian language: "Is that not good? My son was killed by a Pawnee!" After satisfying themselves in a demonstration of this kind they disbanded and went quietly to camp.

A few days after this Leon, a Mexican, who was herding some agency stock just across the river from Darlington was found lying upon the ground, shot through the body. He had been a prisoner among the Indians almost like a slave from the time he was a boy. He belonged to Big Mouth's band, and Big Mouth wishing to appear very friendly to the agent and the white people, had given Leon his freedom.

Upon examination it was found that the one who did the

shooting had secreted himself behind a bunch of willows near which his victim was sure to pass while returning from his dinner. It was soon discovered that Parker, an Arapahoe, had done the shooting. No excuse was given for it that was any-way satisfactory. Those of us who were carefully studying the Indian character were satisfied that the shooting was done to put the white people more in awe of the Indians and to make us fear them, so that we would the more readily comply with their demands, which were at times very unreasonable, and fell hard upon the agent and his white employees. Leon had a spotted horse which he called his war or buffalo horse. Leon was killed on Saturday and on Sunday he was buried, and his horse shot over his grave in order that its spirit might accompany his master to the happy hunting grounds.

About this time while I was at work on a house in the agency, I heard several shots fired and a moment later the sound of bullets striking the building. I looked out and saw Fred Williams, a young man who was hauling sand, driving like mad, while a young Indian standing behind the wagon was shooting at him with a revolver. After having emptied his weapon, the young warrior leisurely marched back to camp.

Upon inquiry it developed that a lot of camp boys were hanging on the wagon (which was heavily loaded), and young Williams motioned them to get off. As they paid no attention to his orders he drove them from the load. They ran back to camp and told of it, and young White Bear ran out and began to shoot as before stated.

Agent Miles let the matter pass, not seeing his way to punishment at the time, and this encouraged the reckless members of the tribe to be bolder and more arbitrary than before and occasionally a young man in bravado would ride up to an employe's house and demand that the woman of the house bring him a drink of water. The agent had procured some peach trees. After they were nicely set out, some Indians got over in the ground and began pulling them up. Upon being asked why they did this, they replied, "We are trying to find out what you are sticking those sticks in the ground for."

Three men who were taking care of the agency cattle, and who lived about a mile and a half south of the agency, were frequently abused and mistreated by the young braves, but submitted to it in accordance with the Quaker idea that they must offer no resistance, but always be pleasant and friendly.

One day an Indian rode up to their cook shanty, where Mr. Bunk, the cook, was mixing a batch of bread. His hands were in the dough at the time, and the Indian while sitting on his horse at the door ordered Bunk to bring him a drink of water. Bunk told him there was no water in the bucket, and that his hands were in the dough, and that if he waited until he got the bread mixed he would go and fetch the water.

The Indian drew his six-shooter and fired five shots into the water bucket and then rode off.

About this time I was plastering a house at the agency, and a party of men came in, some fifteen or more, and began to scratch on the freshly plastered wall. I forbade them to do so, and they ran upstairs, and as I started to follow them, one of them who had a tomahawk in his hand, motioned for me to come on, that when I got near enough he would kill me.

As I did not care to die just at that time I stepped back

and fastened the door and went on with my work. Soon I heard them coming down stairs and when they reached the landing, they began to pound on the door wishing to get out. John Williams, the agency blacksmith, was passing and I called to him to come in. I asked him to let the Indians out one at a time until they were all out, which he said he would do. He stood at the door and as the first Indian passed out he quickly shut it again. I took the first chap by his long hair and jerked him to the door and threw him out. He got up and went on a run to camp. I served the second in the same way and so on until the last one had been slammed through the doorway. Williams and I expected nothing else than that the whole camp would return to punish us for the way the young men had been treated, but nothing happened.

I was very curious to know the reason of it and several years after, when I was better acquainted with these people, and had their confidence, I brought the incident up one day with a friendly Indian, and asked him why it was that the Indians at the time did not retaliate upon me. He replied: "The young men probably went to the building to get up a fuss with you and were ashamed to tell that two white men, without arms, had whipped them without suffering any injury. They would have been laughed at had they complained."

Chapter IV

MY BATTLE

WITH THE BOYS

AFTER CERTAIN PRISONERS were taken away in 1875, the majority of the Cheyennes became friendly and expressed a willingness to follow the white man's ways. Bull Bear and White Shield, who were among the first chiefs to come in from the warpath and who had not been held as prisoners of war, agreed to put their children in school, and were the first of the Cheyennes to do so. Bull Bear, not wishing to have his sons behind any of the Arapahoe boys, gave me a fine buffalo robe which he asked me to exchange for cattle, so that his boy, in whom he took great pride, would be put on equality with those Arapahoe boys who were raising cattle. I sold the robe for $12.00 and bought two yearling heifers which gave his son a start as a stockman.

The Cheyennes having lost most of their ponies were now dependent entirely upon the rations which the government issued to them, and to make matters worse they were not allowed to leave the agency even on foot for the purpose of

---

hunting buffalo. This confinement about the agency was very irksome to these Arabs of the level country, and when the agent laid the matter before them they all expressed a willingness to plow and plant, but there were at the time very few tools available for their use, and the supply of seed was inadequate.

There were, at this time, about 150 acres of land which had been broken up for agency use, and this was turned over to them. They went to work upon it, using the few plows available, and in some cases began to dig up the ground with hoes and spades, or even butcher knives. Having no wagons they carried the posts for the fences on their backs or dragged them along the ground with lariat ropes, and so enclosed the land. They succeeded in raising a good crop that year and were peaceable and entirely obedient to the agent's orders and were getting along very nicely when the plan for moving into this territory other Indians from the North began to be discussed. It was proposed to gather the Indians into one big reservation and form an Indian Territory, where the red people could all live together. It was thought the government could handle them in one body with better results than when they were scattered out over so much territory. This plan included bringing the Northern Cheyennes as well as the Northern Arapahoes down to the Cheyenne and Arapahoe reservation. After the Custer battle, in which many Cheyennes were engaged, the authorities considered that if the warlike Northern Cheyennes were brought down to the agency and affiliated with their southern brethren, it would be easier to get them to take up the white man's ways. The northern division of the tribe agreed to do this, but as they afterwards said, it was with the understanding that if they did not like it in the South they could return North. At any rate, they were moved down to Darlington.

But when they reached there, instead of falling in with the agent's ideas of farming and raising corn, they began to give dances and to sing warsongs and to tell of their exploits and battles, and soon had their southern brethren very unsettled and dissatisfied. When they heard that some of the Southern Cheyennes had put their children in school and that some of these boys had been whipped by white men, they began to make fun of the parents and ridiculed them. "Will you let the white wolves whip your boys?" And when the large boys went to camp the young men called them squaws and taunted them with cowardice and with wearing short hair like Negroes.

All this was very galling to the boys. While they liked to go to camp and hear the stories of the warpath, they disliked the never-failing jeering of their northern cousins.

To call a Cheyenne a white man was considered one of the worst insults that could be offered him.

Up to this time the largest boys of the school had been very obedient, but the persecution which they received from the camp Indians made them feel that they were being imposed upon and in order to preserve their standing as young warriors they began to think they must do something to redeem themselves. They began to be insubordinate and very hard to manage.

I learned that they had been counseling with some of the young men in camp who had promised to back them up in resistance to my authority. It was our second summer and we were very busy putting up hay and doing farm work. I was working with the boys and one night when I told them to march up to their rooms they turned and went out in front of the house and began making cigarettes, paying no attention to me. There were nearly twenty in this bunch, and when I followed them out and ordered them to put away their cigarettes and go to bed, one of the large boys deliberately raised his cigarette to his lips. Again I repeated my order: "Boys, go to bed."

Max cried out in Arapahoe, "Now is the time, boys, to let him see who is boss." Upon this the whole crowd rushed toward me. I saw that war was declared. With a leap I knocked Max down, and facing the others I cried out: "Come on, boys, and we will see who is boss," but when they saw Max go tumbling to the ground, they hesitated, and as I walked towards the nearest boy with my fist drawn back, they all turned and went to bed without further resistance, Max the meekest one of the crowd.

The next evening two of the boys got to fighting at the table, and I took them both outside the door and gave them a sound drubbing. That night when they were going to their rooms to retire one of the teachers stood in the hall with a lighted candle in her hand to light them to their rooms. One of the large boys blew out the light. She lighted it again, and he blew it out a second time. By this time I had come up. I took him by the collar and shoved him into his sleeping room. The other boys followed and stood in a group while William the culprit turned around and said: "Tomorrow morning you and I will fight and when the fight is over you won't be alive." I told him the fight might as well take place there and if he was ready we would begin.

Another boy stepped up and said in an excited manner: "All right we will all begin, I shall fight right along with William."

"Very well," I replied, "when you are ready the fight will begin." When I said this several revolvers were pulled out and cocked. This was a little more war than I had anticipated. I felt the need of consulting with the agent before I called their bluff. I retreated, shutting the door, taking the light with me. Hurrying to the room where our cook, a young man, was sleeping, I asked him to go and sit in my room opposite where the boys were and see that no one left the room until I came back, that I was going to see the agent.

I did not tell him anything about what had taken place, thinking it best not to alarm him.

I found the agent suffering from an attack of neuralgia, scarcely able to converse, much less to advise with me. I stated the case to him and asked what I had better do.

He said: "I can't advise you. The Indians are on the point of breaking out already. The Northern Cheyennes have worked our Indians up to a state of dangerous excitement and I don't know what to do. The military stands ready to take charge of them should they break out again, and in all probability the agency will be abolished. Under the circumstances I can give no advice. The Indians have probably instigated this insurrection of the large boys to afford an excuse for going on the warpath again, and the troops we have are not sufficient to protect us from attack. I can't offer any suggestions or give any instructions in regard to what you are to do in this matter; use your own judgment."

Meanwhile Mr. Turnbaw (whom I had left in charge of

the boys) hearing a great deal of noise and talking in the room thought he would go to the door and tell them to be quiet. When he stepped to the door with the candle in his hand, several revolvers were drawn and cocked. He shut the door and went back and sat down in my room waiting my return.

I saw that the youngsters were fully decided to fight. I concluded not to bother them as long as they did not try to leave the room. Setting my door wide open, I put a chair across the threshold, so that any one entering there in the dark would fall and awaken me, and loading the magazine of my Winchester, I placed it at the head of my bed, and lay down for a nap.

Some time during the night I heard some one fall over the chair in my room. He fell flat upon the carpet, but with sufficient noise to awaken me. I instantly sprang out of bed and struck a match just in time to see him fall over the chair again trying to get out of sight. I could not tell which one of the boys it was, but I followed him with my Winchester in one hand and a lighted match in the other. As I glanced around the room every boy seemed to be sleeping. I knew that they were playing 'possum, but my best policy was to let them think I was deceived. I returned to my bed and remained until the usual time for rising, when I got up and rang the rising bell and began the day's work as if nothing unusual had happened to me. I roused the boys for their morning work and got them ready for breakfast as usual, making no allusion to the scenes of the evening before until after breakfast. I then said: "Go to the play room and remain seated there until I come from my breakfast."

When I had finished my meal I went to the play room where I found them all seated and looking very sullen. I did not know just how many were committed to this insurrection, so I thought the first thing for me to do was to find out. Addressing Dan Tucker, one of the largest boys, I asked him if he wanted to fight with me. He said he did not. I asked the same question to another herder. He said no. I told him to go about his work. The boys farther down called out to them, "You're a squaw." Finally the third one, when I asked him whether he wanted to fight with me or not said, "I don't know." The fourth answered in the same words, and so on down the line until about eighteen boys had replied that they did not know whether they wanted to fight with me or not. I told them in that case I wanted them all to go to the school room. They rose and I marched them into the school and locked the door, and put down the blinds.

Singling out one of the boys who had come to school in a very pitiable condition, his face covered with loathsome scabs and sores, and who owed me everything in the world because I had saved his life, and who had never up to this time been disobedient or wilful, I said, "Homer, I understand these boys all want to fight me, and one of the boys told me that when the fight was over I would not be alive. Now I saw you among the others, and it called to my mind the condition you were in when you came to this school. I am thinking how I worked over your sores, trying to get you well. You ought to know what a job it was to do this and how long it took me and how faithful I worked to cure you. Now you want to fight with me and kill me? Very well, I want you to be the first boy to fight me. Suppose I had wanted to kill you or wished harm to befall you in any way, wouldn't I have left you all covered with awful sores? Well, now we will fight."

When I was talking to him I saw the tears begin to course down his cheeks.

Turning to another boy whom I had nursed through a very serious illness, sitting by his bed through the long nights, I said: "You whom I nursed and bathed and fed—you can be the second boy to fight me." He, too, became very much changed in his appearance and moved uneasily in his seat. Glancing around the room I could easily distinguish the ring leaders, for as they saw these boys cringing under my talk they grew restless and at last one of them said: "We would have nothing against you if you did not whip us. When we go to camp the young men in camp call us squaws and make fun of us, and they said we were foolish to let one white man beat us when if we would stick together we could easily whip you. They said if we needed any help we could run out to camp and they would help us there."

I told them if that was all that troubled them, the matter could very easily be settled. "I do not whip you unless you disobey the rules of the school. The way to do is to obey all the rules and I will not whip you. If you disobey I have a right to punish you. How is it in camp? When an Indian does not obey the rules of the chief or the Dog Soldiers he is punished. You know that. Well, I am the chief here and I have a right to enforce discipline. Don't you see that this is true?" They replied, "Yes, we see that." I said, "Well, all you have to do is to make up your minds to obey all my rules, and I will see that none of you are whipped."

This they promised to do. I then shook hands with each

one of them and told them to go to their work and also get ready for school. And another critical moment was passed safely.

Through this summer and autumn, things remained very much the same. The agency people kept constantly on the alert. We had learned to trust the Arapahoes and yet some of them, as they saw how much we depended upon them, became very exacting and expected a great many privileges. They took the liberty of entering employees' houses whenever they chose to do so, and were often annoying. They felt we owed them a great deal—and we did—but we did not enjoy their presumption.

When the first of September arrived, the question of opening the boarding school, which had been closed for two months, came up, and even the Arapahoes who were friendly, did not conceal the fact that they had no friendship for the school. Some of them told the children that the white people intended to take the school-house with all the children in it and take it away off and they would never see their folks again.

This caused the pupils to run away to camp and it would be several days before they could be gathered up again. The young men who had nothing else to do put in a good share of their time annoying the school, making it very difficult for the teachers.

After the doctor's son had been killed it was evident that the young men who killed him had been looking for the superintendent of the school, and Henry King, the superintendent, thinking that the good to be accomplished did not justify the risk being taken, resigned and left for his home in Indiana. It was impossible to get a competent person to come to the agency and take the position, and Mrs. Miles asked the agent why he didn't appoint me to take temporary charge. In this way I entered the service. Upon entering the school, I found about twelve or fifteen children who came only in the fore-noon, and ran wild in camp the rest of the day.

In order to keep them in school the superintendent had been forced to watch them constantly until school time, and he dared not let them out until the bell rang for dinner, for fear he would not see them again. After dinner they were ac-customed to scatter out, the boys with their bows and arrows and the girls to camp, to be seen no more until supper time. After supper they were marched into a play room, where they were locked up until a short time before they were sent to bed.

I found the work very hard and confining, and from day to day could see no progress or advancement among the pupils. The outside Indians were very troublesome. They came into the school-house, into the dining room—in fact any part of the house where work was carried on, and sat around and even lay down on the floor. After things had gone on this way for a few days I went to the agent and said: "I don't care to stay at the school any longer, I would rather lay stone or do any kind of mason work than be a superintendent. If any good was being accomplished I would not complain, and I wouldn't give it up, but I can't see that we are making any headway, and unless there is a change in regard to manage-ment, and methods used, I can not see how there can be any progress."

"Have you any changes to propose?" he asked.

I told him that I had, and among other things I said: "The young men should be kept entirely away from the school;

older Indians themselves should not be allowed to come into the building except by permission or under certain restrictions."

He said, "It is all very well to have such rules, but I do not see how we are going to enforce them."

I told him if I could have full authority to do so, I would see that the necessary rules were enforced.

"I am afraid that an attempt to carry out your plans would cause the Arapahoes, who are now friendly, to become our enemies and that some one might be killed as the result.

I told him if I undertook the work I had suggested I would take all the responsibility and risk of doing so, and that no other person should be blamed for what I had done.

Mrs. Miles recommended the agent to let me try my plan; thereupon I was given full charge of the school. On the following night when the employees and children were assembled the agent came to the school-house and told them all that I was to have entire charge of the school and employees, and whatever rules I made he would sustain. I then laid down some rules in a general way and said the following morning they would be put in operation. Among my rules there was: "No camp Indians will be allowed in the dining room at meal times, and none of them will be fed from the dining room table. All camp Indians visiting the school will confine themselves to the children's play room. They will not be allowed to run over the house at will."

The matron and other employees were very much wrought up over these radical changes in respect to conduct. They assured me that I could not carry them out and that if I locked the Indians out of the dining room they would tear the house down.

I told them if we could not keep them out of the dining room, the house might as well be torn down.

The Indians, as a rule, did not get up early enough to bother us at breakfast or before school, but at dinner they were generally on hand in crowds. When dinner was about ready, I locked the outside dining room door and brought the children into the dining room from the play room. Looking out a little later I saw five Indians coming out of their lodge near by. They had started promptly at the ringing of the bell, intending, no doubt, to sit down at the first table and enjoy a good square meal, but when they reached the dining room door, which they usually entered, they found it locked. They kicked and hammered a while, being very indignant at my trick. After the children were seated I unlocked the door, and the Indians who were standing on the door-step undertook to push in. I grabbed the first one, a man named White Crow, by the arm and the back of the neck and gave him a whirl which sent him sprawling on the ground. The others stood back to see what he would do. He jumped up and gathered his blanket around him, taking the edge between his teeth, with his hand on the knife in his belt. He marched up in front of me, straightened up and said in a very dignified way, and rather vehemently, "I am a chief."

I had no knife to take hold of, so I doubled up my fist and shook it in his face and said, "I am a chief, too. You are a chief in camp and I am a chief in school."

He said, "I and all the Arapahoes are friends of the school. We were just coming over to get our dinner. I do not know why you treat me so."

"You know that the rations for the grown Indians are issued

from the Commissary," I replied. "But the rations for the children are sent to the school. It is my duty to see that the children get what belongs to them and plenty to eat. Heretofore you Indians from the camp have come to the dining room filling up the tables and eating up the food when the children did not have enough to eat. This will not occur again while I am here."

White Crow commenced to look less stern and his hand dropped from the handle of his knife. As he stepped back from confronting me, his companions laughed and Yellow Horse said, "Do you say that we can not have anything to eat from your table? We know that after the children are through eating there will be scraps of meat and pieces of bread left that you will throw in the barrel outside the house and it will be given to the hogs. We are your friends, and we have come to see you. Will you treat the hogs better than you do us?"

"No," I replied, "if you will go around into the play room and sit down and remain there until after the children are through eating, I will gather up the best that is left and bring it to you."

"Very good," he replied, "you are a new chief. We have not learned your ways, and if that is your way of treating your friends we will put up with it."

They then went around to the playroom and took seats, and after the children were through eating I gathered up some of the meat and bread in a pan and carried it in and gave it to them. They said, "Now since we are better acquainted, we know how you feed your friends when they come to see you. You feed them at the back door like dogs. We know now what to expect when we come to make a friendly call."

After shaking hands and bidding me good-bye they again said: "We will tell it around through camp so that everybody will know how you treat your friends when they come to see you."

"All right," I said, "I hope you will. It is my duty to look out for the children first, and remember my friends afterwards."

After this I had very little trouble to get the Indians out of the dining room, for they had learned that when I forbade them to go into the sewing room or any part of the house I meant what I said.

Chapter V

I BECOME A

MEDICINE MAN

THERE WAS A WELL at the south end of the school building which afforded scarcely water enough for the use of the school. Every day large crowds of young Arapahoes used to gather on a level piece of ground near the school to race their ponies. As the weather was warm, they came thronging to the well to get water. They generally rode up ten or twenty in a bunch and lingered round the well for some time enjoying the cool water, which they pumped out by hand. The pump was a great novelty to them; they pumped water just to see it run. In this way they made a large mudhole near the well which was not only unsightly but a menace to the health of the school. I felt very uneasy about this, for the young men were ready to avail themselves of any excuse for a row with the school superintendent. I thought the matter over very carefully before I decided what course to take.

One morning I told the employees that I intended to stop the Indians from watering at the well. They all agreed that it would be impossible for me to do so, that it would be unwise for me to undertake it, as they were sure there would be a fight if I tried to enforce such an order.

"Very well," I said, "there will be a fight, for I will not allow them to commit this nuisance any longer."

About 10 o'clock next day they began to assemble at the race tracks, as usual, and soon after two young fellows came riding towards the well. I went out to meet them and told them as pleasantly as I could of the harm they were doing. "If you want a drink tie your horses some distance from the well."

They laughed at the idea of complying with any directions of mine and began to urge their horses past me. They were riding side by side and I was directly in their path. I repeated several times the order for them to stop, which they did not heed, and when they reached me I grabbed their horses by the bits and set them back on their haunches with all the strength I had.

They looked at one another and then at me, and finally rode back to the crowd at the race track. I watched them with some anxiety to know what would be the outcome of my opposition. I saw the crowd of young men congregate around them and finally one man rode out a few rods from the throng and looked back as if calling on the others to follow.

Soon another joined him and then another and at last a crowd of fourteen braves, all of them armed with either guns or bows and arrows, rode directly toward me. When they were close enough for me to see their countenances they appeared very determined and very resolute.

I met them a few rods from the well and commanded

them to stop. They came on without hesitating, but I took my position in front of them and when they reached me I seized the leader's horse by the bridle. Every Indian grabbed his weapon and drew it upon me. I held to the horse's bit, forcing him back.

At this moment, Casper Keller, a young man who was cooking for the school ran out on the steps and asked if there was anything he could do to help me.

"Yes, go in and bring your six-shooter and your cartridge belt." He rushed into the kitchen and came out with his six-shooter in great haste. The Indians were still covering me with their weapons, but it was plain that Keller's movements had created some uneasiness among them. When he came out loading his revolver in their sight, I let go the bit of the horse I was holding and grabbed a piece of fence board, which lay on the ground near me, and flailed that crowd of Indians with every ounce of muscle in me. They could not stand my blows. Wheeling their horses swiftly they went back to the race track much faster than they came. My sudden attack had taken them and their ponies by surprise.

I heard nothing more of this affair, as the young men were ashamed to make any talk about it, or to admit that they had been turned back by two white men, one of them without arms, but I shall never forget the minute of time which elapsed while I held the horse and Keller was loading his revolver. As I glanced up at the house and saw the teachers standing at the windows looking out with white faces, it seemed as if I had precipitated a massacre.

The next problem was how to prevent the children from running to camp in the afternoon. I laid this matter before

Bear Woman (Cheyenne) beading a pair of moccasins in the
Mission work room, Mohonk Lodge, Colony, 1900.

the agent, and asked him if he did not think that by calling
a council of the chiefs and showing them the necessity of
keeping the children in school that they would help us.

The agent said he thought this a good plan, and called
a council of the chiefs and laid the matter before them. He
told them how bad it was to have their children running to
camp at their own will. "The children disregard the rules of
the school; they will not mind those placed over them, and
I want to have you use your influence in making them obedient and more punctual in the future."

The chiefs replied, "In camp we turn the government and
management of the children over to the medicine men. The
children obey them and we do not have to bother with them.
We are chiefs and have charge of the soldiers and the management of tribal affairs. We cannot bother ourselves with
the discipline of children. You better get a medicine man to
run your school. Let him manage the children." This was all
the satisfaction the agent got from his council.

But when I called at his office and he told me what the
Indians had said, I remarked, "They will find a medicine man
is running the school." They had given me an idea.

Among the red men a medicine man is one who can do
things which seem miraculous to the rest of the tribe. I determined on surprising them. Some years before I had learned
a great many sleight-of-hand tricks and had practiced them
to some extent. I had even given exhibitions of my skill in
this line to entertain small parties of my friends. I now hastened to the blacksmith and gave him directions for making
some "properties," including a knife and some rings. I also
sent to Wichita, Kansas, to get other apparatus which would

51

aid me in my "conjuring." As soon as I had gathered these things together, I was prepared to show the scholars a thing or two that would bewilder them.

One day a girl ran away from school and I followed her and found her in the company of her father and mother who were taking her away to camp.

I had to take hold of her and put her on my horse and hold her there, while I led the horse back to school. The father and mother followed along, and I could see that they intended to steal her away again at the first opportunity. She was about fourteen years old and very stubborn. It was evident that her parents sympathized with her wish to go to camp, but they found no opportunity for taking her away after supper, and when it became dark they were still in the play room waiting. Leaving an employee to watch her until I came down, I went to my room and got my trick-knife, which I handed to the father of the girl. "Examine that," I said.

He did not understand why I wished him to do this, but he took it. I adjusted a duplicate blade on my left wrist, and when they handed the knife back to me I raised it and apparently plunged it through my left wrist. Instead I dropped it into my pocket and substituted the duplicate, which to all appearance, had gone through my wrist.

As I thrust my arm towards them with the knife through it, the old man commenced to back away. I followed him holding the arm out and taking hold of the handle of the knife, moved it back and forwards. This more than anything else convinced him that it had gone through my arm. Much frightened, they both ran out of the door and started for camp as fast as they could go. I turned to the school children who were all very excited, and as I held out my right hand the children rushed up eager to examine the wound, but could find no scar. They all exclaimed, "Medicine Man!" And in a few hours the news spread over the camp that I was a conjuror and could stick a knife through my wrist and suffer no harm.

About this time our well went dry and myself and two agency employees took out the wall to dig it deeper. The last four or five feet of digging was in quicksand, which caved in, leaving quite a cavity. Finally, after digging as far as we dared on account of the quicksand, I went into the well to lay the wall while two employees prepared to let the rock down to me. The bucket which they were using was a square box holding about a barrel. After they had filled this box with rock, and were about to let it down, the rope came untied, and the bucket fell a distance of more than thirty feet.

I saw the bucket when it started, and fell back into the cavity which had resulted from the quicksand, and thus escaped being killed. However a corner of the box struck me, cutting a gash in my forehead and smashing my nose. This caused the blood to run profusely, making a black streak from my shoulder to my knee, besides giving me quite a shock. The bucket and rock dropped to the bottom of the well where there was a few inches of water; the mud and water flew up into the air completely filling the well with flying water and mud. To all appearances it would seem that I had been ground to atoms.

The two men standing on the top of the well ran around crying out: "Oh! Oh! Oh!" and though I was very badly shocked and stunned I was the first to speak. My head was very numb and when I put my finger into the wound it seemed to me that my skull was broken and I could feel my brains.

I told them to let down the rope as I wanted to come out. "My skull is broken," I cried.

They quickly let the rope down, but there was nothing for me to ride up in, as the box was a total wreck. I tied a loop in the end of the rope and put my foot in this, and taking hold of the rope told them to pull away. By this time the blood from my wounds had completely covered me, and there was quite a party of Indians standing around the well who saw me come out. I walked without assistance to the doctor's office where my wounds were dressed. I changed my clothes and in about two hours was back in the well again with very little to show the effects of my accident—the wound being carefully covered with a piece of adhesive plaster which made very little change in my appearance.

The Indians, of course, had gone to camp, and the news of what had happened to the medicine man circulated rapidly, and as they knew nothing about the cavity at the bottom of the well it looked as though the bucket had fallen directly upon me. They said, "The bucket of rock fell upon him and yet he came out and walked away as if not hurt, except he was bleeding."

This established my reputation as a great magician. A few days later when the Indians were at the well again I was standing on the top of the ground, and they inquired why it was that the rock falling on me did not kill me. I told them I would show them. Remembering a principle of natural philosophy stated in my school books, I laid down upon my back and pointed at a flat rock lying near by and told them to place that on my breast.

The rock was as large as two of them could handle, and they objected to laying it on my breast, as they said it would smash me. I told them not to be afraid, but lay it on, which they did. I pointed to a stone-hammer lying near and told them to take that and pound on the rock with it until that had broken the rock. They first commenced pounding very lightly, and as I knew that the heft of the rock was greater than the force of any blow they might strike, I insisted upon their striking the rock as hard as they possibly could. They finally did so and the rock broke in two.

This surprised them very much and they went to camp and told again what they had seen the medicine man do, and this also became the topic of excited conversation around the camp fires.

A little half-breed boy, who told me all the news from camp, came running to me one day and said: "The old men have decided why it is that the rock falling on you and rock which was broken on your breast did not kill you. They say that your magic is in your body and breast and that in your face and head you are not protected. So if any one wanted to kill you they would have to shoot you in the head—if they shot you in the body the bullet would flatten out. They say the reason you were not killed in the well was because you fell on your back and the bucket struck you in the breast, and as you were 'medicine' in the breast, it could not hurt you there, but some of the rock must have fallen on your face and made it bleed, which shows you are not 'medicine' in the face and head."

Chapter VI

I GO TO WAR WITH HIPPY

A CAMP OF RED PEOPLE is like a village—it has all kinds of people in its citizenship. There are men like Big Horse whose word was inviolate and women like Attucker's mother, who broke the bows of her truant boys—but there are also reckless men and mischievous boys to make trouble for their own people as well as for the whites.

There was a peculiar character among our Southern Cheyennes, who had been nick-named "Hippy" because he had been wounded in the hip and had a hitch in his walk on account of it. Hippy was a peculiar character. He was a fool-hardy man, and delighted in doing desperate things that he might be talked about, and even when the Indians were at peace Hippy was always having adventures. Several times he had been shot by white soldiers and by the Utes, and had arrow wounds in different parts of his body. He delighted in displaying these wounds and in relating his many hair-breadth escapes.

Naturally agency life seemed very tame to him, and when the Northern Cheyennes arrived he spent most of his time in camp listening to their account of the Custer battle, and other engagements, and lost no opportunity to display his wounds and recount to them his own deeds of valor. He had two girls in school and frequently called to see them. Now the Indian men were not allowed to go in and sit down in the girls' play room and smoke, neither were the girls allowed in the boys' play room, but Hippy came into the girls' play room one day and began to fill his pipe. I saw him and told him he must go into the boys' play room if he wished to smoke. He said, "I want to talk with my daughters, and as you do not allow the girls to go into the boys' play room, I will sit here and talk to them and take a smoke at the same time."

"You must go into the other room," I repeated. He finally went in but called his girls, telling them to come where he was. I forbade them to do so and Hippy came back into the girls' play room and commenced an insulting harangue. I told him to go out and made a demonstration as if to put him out.

Drawing a knife he growled out, "Come on if you want to put me out of the room."

I said to him, "Hippy, I don't want any trouble with you," and walked to the other side of the room away from him.

Thinking he had me bluffed he followed me up and shook his hands in my face, and said, "Why don't you take hold of me?"

At the same time he had his knife clutched in his hands, apparently ready to strike with it. Seeing that he was determined to have a quarrel, I caught the hand that held the knife with one hand and with the other I took him by the back of the neck and commenced hustling him to the door. He struggled to free the hand that held the knife and resisted my effort, but I had him going. As I neared the door which was then open, he kicked it shut and I could not open it without letting go either of his knife or his neck.

Just when I needed him most, Keller, my cook, came into the room and asked if he could help me in any way.

I told him I did not wish any help in regard to Hippy, but if he would open the door and hold it open I'd be much obliged.

He opened the door and I slammed Hippy through, intending to jump back into the house and shut the door.

Hippy had foreseen the possibility of my doing so, and grimly clutched my coat collar in one hand, so firmly that I could not get free from him. I was forced to hold the hand with the knife. As long as he clung to me it was not necessary for me to hold him.

With my free hand I slipped my coat from my shoulder leaving him holding the collar. He struck at me with the knife, but I was on guard, and evaded the blow, and again seized the hand that held the knife. With a quick shove I sent him tumbling off the porch.

He struck the ground some three feet below the porch floor with stunning force. I jumped upon him and taking him by the throat shut off his wind. After I had choked him until he turned black in the face I loosened my grip and asked him if he would behave himself if I let him get up again.

He replied *"Pewa,"* a Cheyenne word, which means, "Good."

I supposed that he meant to say that he would be good if I let him get up, and released him but kept an eye on him. The minute he rose to his feet he plunged at me with his knife.

I jumped away from him and ran. He followed me closely, striking at me at every step. Being the quicker of the two, I soon gained some ground upon him, and seeing a stone ahead of me lying on the ground I stooped and picked it up and turned and faced him. He saw the stone and stopped about ten feet distant from me. There we faced each other—he with his knife drawn and I with a stone ready to smash him. He dared me to throw the stone.

As the stone was heavy and I knew he could easily dodge it and reach me with his knife, I looked around warily. At this moment I caught sight of a piece of lodge pole about ten feet long lying on the ground near my feet. Dropping the stone I caught up this pole. I then said, "Hippy, the reason I did not throw the stone was because I did not want to kill you, but now if you do not put up your knife and behave yourself I am going to knock you over and pound you with that pole."

He perceived that I could easily swipe him with the pole, and that he could not touch me with his knife. He grew polite. "If you'll throw down your pole I'll put up my knife."

As quickly as he said this I dropped the pole. His word being given he put his knife into its scabbard. I then said, "Come with me to the agent's office."

"All right," said he, "I am ready to do so," and thereupon we started traveling side by side, each one eyeing the other sharply all the way. When we got to the floor of the agent's office we had to climb several steps, and there was only room for one at a time.

"Go ahead," said I.

"No," said Hippy, "you go first."

I said, "Will you follow?"

"Yes, I will come," he replied. I went into the office and Hippy followed me.

Agent Miles was there and I told him briefly what had taken place—how Hippy had drawn his knife upon me, and how we had a fight over it. I told him that several times during the scuffle I could have killed him if I had wished to do so, as I had him in my power, but I did not want to bring any trouble or disturbance upon the agency; therefore I had spared his life. "I will not take any more chances with him," I concluded. "I want to give notice both to the Indians and to the agency that if he comes into my school again, I will kill him at once."

What I had said in regard to the affair the agent had interpreted to Hippy, and the agent asked him if that was a true statement of the case.

"It is," said Hippy calmly. "True in every particular. But I have something to add to it. I want to say that I believe I am going to die from the effects of being thrown from the porch to the ground: I felt something break inside me. I am sure I shall not live long after this, but I shall live long enough to kill Me-o-kany.[1] I will kill him at the first opportunity. I have been placed upon my honor in coming here. He said he would put up his club if I put up my knife, and now I have come to the office I have no more promises to keep. I am free to kill him, and I will do it."

The agent asked me what I thought ought to be done

[1] *Me-o-kany* or *Wo-o-hki-nih*, the name given to John H. Seger by the Cheyennes, meaning Big Nose or Roman Nose.—*Editor.*

in the matter. "Would you advise that Hippy be turned over to the military?" he asked.

My blood was up and I replied, "So far as I am concerned I do not care what you do with him. I can protect myself, and I have given him fair warning of what I shall do in the future in regard to him."

The agent sent a runner to camp asking some of the chiefs to come to his office. Big Horse and White Shield came in response to the summons.

After hearing the case they said, "We are not much surprised at Hippy's actions. He has been that way all his life. He is always doing mean and desperate things, and has made our people a great deal of trouble on account of it. We have no sympathy with him. It is a pity Meokany did not kill him when he had such a good chance."

White Shield said, "It is wiser not to have done so, for Hippy has some sons, who are as foolish as Hippy himself, and they would have taken the life of some white person in retaliation. On this account it is better that you did not kill him. We will take him to camp and will not permit him to come to the agency again. If he does you have our permission to kill him as you have threatened."

They took Hippy to camp and kept him there for some time. He was galled by this confinement, and tried on several occasions to slip away from those guarding him, but they were able to prevent him. On one occasion they had to knock him down to keep him from getting away.

At last he changed his tactics and pretended to be penitent. He begged that he might be allowed to walk around the agency, provided he would not come inside the school grounds. Previous to this, however, he had on several occasions sent messages by the young men, who were ready enough to bring them, that as soon as he could get out of camp he was coming up to the school to kill me. I sent back word that he could not come any too quick, as I had the ball in my gun with which I expected to plug him.

At last he begged permission of his chiefs to go to see his girls. "I'll keep out of the school grounds and take no weapons with me," he said. The chiefs at last consented to lay the matter before the agent and myself to see if we would consent to allow him to come.

The agent left the decision to me and I said, "It don't make any difference how much he comes to the agency, I will not molest him outside of the school grounds, but if he as much as puts his foot inside of the school fence I'll kill him."

He came to the agency every day after this and walked around wistfully till he caught sight of his girls. He called them to him, and they would go to the fence and talk with him, but he did not offer to step inside. These meetings went on in this way for several weeks. I often met him on the streets of the agency, and once or twice he attempted to speak to me, but I turned my head and walked on without reply. On one trip on horseback a mile or two from the agency, I unexpectedly met Hippy. He was surprised; so was I. We eyed each other until we were safely out of gun-shot. As neither of us had a weapon at the time we were in no danger.

Near the close of the term we announced certain closing exercises, and invited all the parents of the children to attend. We were to give them a dinner, in order to win their promise to bring the children back to school, when vacation was over.

In looking forward to this dinner I thought about Hippy's girls—how good and obedient they had been—and my heart softened toward Hippy. I told the agent I would be willing to make an exception in this case and allow Hippy to come in and attend the closing exercises and take his children home with him. When Miles told Hippy that I had invited him to the closing exercises and that he would be allowed inside the school grounds without fearing anything from me, Hippy replied, "My heart is good. Meokany has made me happy, but I would like you to write me a pass to the grounds. I want you to put it in a big envelope so that when I hand it to him he will know it came from headquarters."

This the agent did, and as soon as he entered the school grounds Hippy held the official envelope high over his head like a flag of truce and watched me very carefully until I read the pass from the agent. I then said, "It is all right, you need not fear anything from me this day," which relieved him very much.

He enjoyed his dinner and the exercises very much and when it came time to leave he came and offered me his hand and said: "I want to come again. When will you let me come?"

"Inasmuch as you have obeyed my commands, you have behaved splendidly during the day, and you may call in two weeks."

At the end of the two weeks he was on hand promptly. He stayed an hour or two, visiting with his daughters, and when ready to leave asked: "When can I come again?"

I then said, "I will remove all restrictions upon you so long as you behave properly."

This appeared to be the first time that Hippy had ever been in any way beaten or had come out second best and the Cheyennes guyed him without mercy about it. The Northern Cheyennes (assembled in a large camp about a mile from the agency) were having dances every night, and many of the other Indians gathered there at night to share in the story-telling and fun. The Northern Cheyennes by this time were in full possession of the story of Hippy's encounter with me and whenever he rose to pose as a warrior or a desperate man, some wag always shouted, "How about Johnny Smoker? He laid you out."

This galled him terribly. The Indians after this began to prepare for a Sun Dance, and had invited the Comanches and Kiowas to join them. It happened that Hippy's oldest daughter was detailed in the kitchen at the school and Hippy was hard put to it to furnish his part of the feast. He told his daughter to slip out coffee and sugar and such other provisions as she could bring during the week and when she was allowed to visit her home on Saturday to bring them with her. She obeyed and on Saturday morning after she had started to camp an Arapahoe girl told the matron all about this pilfering. When the matter was brought to my notice I put a boy on a horse and told him to tell Hippy if he did not return the coffee and sugar at once I would deduct what he had taken from his next rations.

The Arapahoe boy reached the camp just as a party had assembled to partake of the feast, which Hippy had intended giving them out of the rations his daughter had stolen. The Arapahoe boy delivered my message to Hippy, accusing his daughter of stealing the rations, and demanded that they be returned at once, otherwise they would be held out from his next ration issue.

This took place in the presence of the guests, and was very humiliating to Hippy. He denied that his daughter had stolen the rations and commanded that his wife should get their own rations that they had drawn the week before and send them to me, and said, "I will come up to see about the matter in the evening.

Towards sunset he came into the school grounds with his face painted up gorgeously. His two wives were with him, also the daughter who had stolen the rations.

I was building a wood-shed near the house and was busy sawing some boards. Hippy and his wife and daughter came and stood by me. The red people all knew that something out of the ordinary was going to happen. All the school came running to see what was going to take place.

Hippy turned to them and said, "Why do you children tell tales on each other? You Arapahoe children should be friends to the Cheyennes. The Cheyennes and Arapahoes have always stood together against the white men. Now you go and inform on my daughter and bring her into trouble when on the other hand you ought to help cover up the things she did. And if she was discovered and punished you ought to all turn in and help her fight this man. If you are not strong enough to whip him we have plenty of warriors in camp who will come in and help you." He then turned to me: "You have brought my family into disgrace. You have accused my daughter of stealing in the presence of the young men whom I had invited to the feast. I now have to make another feast and ask them all in again in order to keep them from throwing the thing up to me and bringing me into ridicule. My daughter has a cow in the school herd and I want to kill it in order to make the feast."

Hippy went on: "Now I want you to put out my daughter's cow to me and I will kill it and make this feast."

I replied, "Your daughter knows on what terms she holds this cow and what the conditions are. I don't need to have anything more to do with it. The herders are instructed what to do in caring for these cattle."

Upon this they held a whispered consultation to one side, and when it was over the daughter, who was a school girl, came up in front of me in a very impudent way, stuck out her tongue at me and said: "yea, yea, yea."

I glanced around as she did this and saw Hippy's two women, on either side of me, with sharp butcher knives in their hands. It was plain they expected me to take hold of the girl or slap her in punishment for her impudence. If I had done so, they would have knifed me. There would have been no witnesses except the school children and themselves, and they would have claimed that I assaulted their daughter and that they killed me in defending her. I saw it would be foolish to bring on any engagement with them, so I dropped my saw and left them.

Going to my room I took off my working clothes, determined to call upon the commanding officer at Fort Reno. Hippy had said to the children, however, at the commencement of our interview that he had seen the commander at the military post and that he had told him he would not take up any quarrel on my account; that he did not expect to take any part in any controversy between me and the Indians.

Schoolboys policing the grounds of the Seger Indian School, Colony, 1900.

I saw that, if this was true, it added a great deal to Hippy's feeling that I would not be protected.

After I had made my toilet I saddled my horse and rode to Fort Reno, leaving Hippy and his two wives and daughter victorious on the school ground.

Calling upon Major John K. Mizner, Fourth Cavalry, who had taken command in 1876, I told him what had taken place at the school. He said, "I can not interfere in any quarrels between you and the Indians. We have only a small force here and the Indians are worked up to a state of excitement where a very small thing might bring on an engagement. They largely outnumber us and might completely overcome us."

I told him that Hippy had said that he had had an interview with him and that he had told him he would not protect me in my course, and that I simply wanted to know whether that was so or not, for I was running the school under contract with the government and was under bonds to do my part; that I was not expected to fight Indians, neither was I expected to put up with the abuse of Indian men like Hippy. "Unless I can be protected in my school work on my own grounds where I have to do the work, I will dismiss my school and ask to be relieved from my contract on the grounds that the troops can not protect me."

As I rose to go he said, "Hold on, I want you to understand that I am willing to protect the people of the agency as long as I have a man to do so, but it seemed to me that our force is altogether too small to risk an attack at this time."

To this I replied: "If that is your view of the case I will lay the matter before the Indian office and claim protection or relief from my contract."

"What do you think ought to be done in this case?" he asked.

"Hippy should be arrested and put into the guardhouse. That will settle the whole matter."

"I am satisfied if I sent a detail of soldiers to the Indian camp and demanded Hippy they would refuse to give him up. In this case I would have to acknowledge my inability to take him, or bring on an engagement with the Indians."

I then said, "If you will accept Hippy at the guardhouse and keep him there I will arrest him myself and bring him over and deliver him to you."

"I don't want you to do that, but if you can get Hippy at the agency when there are very few Indians about and hold him until I can send a detail of soldiers for him, I will take care of him."

"All right; that suits me," I replied. "The first time Hippy comes to Darlington I will send you word and I will see that he is delivered over to your men." Mounting my horse I returned to the agency only to find Hippy and his two wives and his daughter standing in the school grounds, in the same place where I left them."

"Where have you been?" asked Hippy.

I gave no answer.

"What shall my girl do—shall she go to bed or not?"

"She heard the bell ring, didn't she? She knows what she ought to do, and knows that the other children have gone to bed."

"My girl has had no supper."

"She was standing there when the supper bell rang, wasn't she? She knew what she should have done to get her supper."

The girl went to bed and Hippy and his two wives returned to camp.

The next day he came to the agency, evidently to find out what I had gone away for. He inferred I had been to the Post, and he was very anxious to know what I had done. Upon reaching the agency he went to the blacksmith shop and asked the smith if he knew what I had gone to the Fort for. The blacksmith said he did not know exactly what I had gone for. Hippy then went to the agent's office.

I was watching his movements, and as soon as he went into the office I sent a courier to the Post telling the commander to send his detail of soldiers for Hippy. I then instructed Mr. Williams, the blacksmith, to stand ready to detain Hippy until the soldiers came, providing he left the Commissary.

When Hippy entered the agent's office, Miles was talking with Ed. Guery,[2] a half-breed Cheyenne, who not only understood Cheyenne, but also understood and spoke Comanche. When Hippy entered the agent shook hands with him and told him to be seated. The agent asked him if he would not like some rations to take home with him. Hippy said he would. The agent told the Commissary clerk to go into the Commissary and put up some rations for Hippy. The clerk understood very well that he was to be gone as long about it as possible.

While Hippy was sitting in the agent's office a Comanche Indian came in and sat down beside him and entered into a conversation with him, which was overheard by Guery, the

---

[2] Edmond Guerrier, the well-known scout and interpreter, for whom was named the town of Geary, Oklahoma, near which he still lives.

half-breed interpreter. Hippy related what had taken place and told him I had been to the Post but he didn't know what for, though he thought I had failed to get help.

"Everybody is very friendly to me this morning, and even the agent is more cordial than usual. He has just sent his clerk into the Commissary for some rations for me. I have got them all scared. After this when I want anything to eat, all I have to do is to make some threat and I can get anything I want. I wish you would come to my camp during your visit, for I will have plenty to eat and know now how to get more when I need it."

About this time the Commissary clerk, glancing from the window, saw the ambulance and the detail of soldiers coming from the Post. He brought the rations out and gave them to Hippy, who as he left the office turned to the Comanche and said, "Come right up to my place, I will go on and give the rations to my squaw and have her get the dinner ready."

He went out of the office alone, but he seemed to think that he might get some further information from the blacksmith to satisfy himself why it was that the agency people were so friendly with him after his trouble. He did not see the soldiers coming, but the blacksmith did and knew the importance of keeping Hippy's face away from the Fort, so when he asked the blacksmith again whether he had heard anything more about my trip to the Post the night before, the blacksmith, as if he wished to get a drink, told him if he would come over to a well which was a short distance from the shop, he would tell him all about it.

They started for the well, keeping their backs to the coming soldiers, and stepped behind the house to get a drink, completely shutting the soldiers and ambulance from Hippy's view. All at once the ambulance drew up near the well and a file of soldiers jumped out and surrounded Hippy, with their bayonets pointed towards him.

Hippy when he saw the soldiers asked, "What are these soldiers after?"

Williams replied, "I think they are after you."

"I have not so much as a knife to defend myself. If I had, they would not take me alive," he said.

By this time the soldiers had their bayonets presented and they pointed towards the ambulance, telling him to get into it. He did not start until he was pricked pretty sharply by the bayonets. He climbed into the ambulance, the soldiers following him. They took their seats on each side of him, and the team was quickly turned towards the Post and driven rapidly away.

Just as they were leaving the agency, Hippy seized a gun in each hand and tried to jump out of the ambulance, but the points of the bayonets were put against him and he was pushed down in his seat. This quieted his spirit and he was safely landed in the guardhouse without creating any excitement among the Indians, as they were all gathered at camp where the Sun Dance was in progress.

Hippy's circle of friends among the Indians was not very large, since they were for the most part law-abiding and peaceful, and his arrest did not create the excitement that was expected by the commanding officer. But the humiliation of being put in the guardhouse and the second time being beaten by "Johnny Smoker" so worked upon Hippy's feelings that he fell ill, and the commanding officer fearing he would die sent a courier to me asking if I were willing to let him be turned loose to die in camp.

I told him that it did not matter to me, that as long as he stayed out of the school grounds it would be all right. If they would have him promise to keep out of the school I did not care. They let him out of the guardhouse to die, but as soon as he was out he changed his mind about dying and concluded to get well. As soon as he had recovered so that he could walk he came to the school grounds and to my surprise one day I stepped out on the porch to find Hippy sitting there. I seized him and dragged him off the grounds and threw him outside the fence and gave him a kick and told him the next time he came on the school grounds I would kill him.

He lay there for some time, but slowly got up and went to camp. He made no attempt to come to school again without my permission, but this did not end his plotting against me, for as soon as he had gotten his health he organized a party of his own boys and relatives for the purpose of killing me. They talked the matter over night after night, and every night a party of young men rode before the school building and sat in groups on their ponies with their blankets drawn over their heads, every one of them being armed. Several days in succession I saw this party congregate in front of the building and one day I asked the school children if they knew what they were there for. A little girl who was a great favorite of mine, and who came to our room quite frequently to help my wife about her work, said she could tell me, but I must not let anyone know who told me. She said, "They are young men Hippy has got to try to kill you, they are watching to see when you go off some place away from the school building, where you will be out of sight from the white folks, when they will follow and kill you. You better not go alone while they are watching you."

I was pretty busy in the hayfield, leaving the children who had remained with us to the matron and teachers. We had no trouble with run-aways for a long time, and it was a great surprise to me when one night I came home from the hayfield to find that four or five of our children had run off to camp. I sent an Arapahoe boy after them but he returned without them and said they would not come.

I was too busy to go after them myself, if I could help it, so I went to my work without bringing them back. The next night when I came home, it was reported that fourteen more of the children had scampered back to their parents. I turned to Dan Tucker, one of our largest school boys, and one who was then herding the issue cattle, "Dan, saddle up my horse; after supper I'll go after them myself."

"You better send me and Neatha after them."

"No," I replied, "I have sent after them before and did not get them—I will go this time myself."

"Let Neatha and me go with you then."

I consented to this and after I had eaten my supper and was ready to start, the boys asked me to hold their horses in order that they might get their revolvers. As herders they were allowed to carry revolvers. Supposing they wished to show off with their revolvers, and knowing that the camp we were going to was a very large one with a big dance going on, I was not surprised that they wished to take their revolvers along, as it was customary at that time for Indians to keep their arms by their sides. We rode up to a bonfire in the center of the camp, where a large number of Indians had congregated preparatory for a dance, and I looked around for the children, but could not see them.

Dan then said, "Let Neatha and me go around camp and look for the children and see where they are; then we will come and tell you and you can come and get them. If you should go with us the children would see you before you saw them, and they would hide away and then you would not get them."

I thought the idea a good one, and told them I would remain at the fire until they returned. As soon as the boys were gone a party of some twenty-five or thirty young men gathered around me, all with their blankets over their heads, and acted as if they meditated evil to me. As I had no weapon with me, I thought it safer to be on the ground, so I slid from my horse and stood in front of them. The Indians gathered on one side of me and one young man in walking past me ran against me. I treated this as a joke, though I knew it was intentional, made with the idea of provoking resistance on my part. Soon another young man passed me and gave me a shove much harder than the first one had done. This was too large a crowd for me, so I mounted my horse and started after my herd boys. I had not gone far until I met the boys coming back, and I asked them if they had found the children. They looked very serious and said, "Yes, they are down at Hippy's camp near the river. The children are there, but there are a lot of young men there and they are all armed and Hippy is mad and the young men are angry too, and told us to come back and send you down there, but for us not to come with you."

After they had delivered their message I told them I was going down to Hippy's camp.

They said. "You had better not go. Hippy is mad; he told us that he was going to kill you."

I told them I was just as mad as Hippy, and that I was going after those children.

"Well, if you are going we are going along with you," they said.

I told them they could go if they chose to, but if they were afraid to go they might stay back. They made no reply, but one of them rode on each side of me, until we reached Hippy's camp. I took in the situation at a glance, for there sat Hippy with a gun across his lap, surrounded by four or five young men with guns by their sides. Hippy was filling his pipe preparatory to smoking.

Knowing the Indian customs as I did, I knew that when they are about to undertake a desperate act they take a smoke first, if possible, and that while they are smoking they consider the plan of this undertaking in all its details, and that when the smoke is finished, if they are still resolved to carry out their plan, the one who is their leader gives the signal. I knew they would not act immediately. I rode up calmly, and said, "How" to them, to which they did not respond. I got down from my horse and stood in front of Hippy in easy reach of him. I was so intent and occupied with what I should do myself that I paid no attention to what the boys were doing, but they dismounted and took their places by my side, one on my right and one on my left, with their six-shooters in their hands.

I did not see them do this, as my attention was upon

Hippy, from whom I knew the signal for action would come. I believed I could snatch his gun away from him and kill him and jump into the bushes before the others could fire. After settling upon this plan I stood waiting for the smoke to be finished. After the pipe had passed around and its contents were consumed, the pipe again came back to Hippy. The critical moment had arrived.

Hippy, instead of giving the signal as I expected him to do, turned to the Arapahoe boys and said, "What are you here for? Did I not tell you to stay away? Did I not tell you I wanted to kill this white man? Don't you know that the Cheyennes and Arapahoes are friends while the white men are our enemies? Don't you know that we have always been against the white man; why do you stand by this man against us?"

When Hippy began to talk I knew that there was no immediate danger. I glanced at the boys when he addressed them, and took in the situation. They were standing resolutely by my side with their revolvers in their hands, with stern resolution on their dark faces. They were brave as lions, and my heart went out to them.

When Hippy had ended his tirade Dan Tucker replied, "It is true the Arapahoes and Cheyennes are friends. Is it not also true that we are at peace with the white people? We are not at the present time on the warpath against them and it is not our way to fight them and kill them when we have made peace with them. We are Arapahoe boys, and we have been taught by our parents and chiefs to always obey our chiefs, and when our parents and chiefs put us in this school they said 'Johnny Smoker is your chief—you must obey him and be true to him as you would be to a chief of your own tribe.' We are now obeying the instructions of our chiefs, and you have no right to question our conduct in doing so. We are here in obedience to this man's instructions and we will stay by him and fight with him if necessary."

Hippy then turned to me and asked, "Why do you whip these children?"

I replied, "I have not whipped them, as these boys know, and if you bring the children out before me they will tell you so."

"Then why were they crying as far as I could hear them when I came to camp?"

"They were probably crying because they knew they would be whipped when they returned to school. They have run away from school and they know when they return I will whip them for running away."

He said, "If you are going to whip those children we will not take them back to school."

"I have come after those children and I will take them back and I will whip them. I am now ready to go and I want you to bring them out of the lodge or I will," I insisted.

"I will bring them out of the lodge and let you take them back to school if you promise not to whip them."

"I *shall* whip them," I declared.

"You must not whip my little girl. She is a timid little thing and is afraid, and will suffer more from the fear of being whipped than in taking the whipping."

"I will whip your little girl," I said, with all the sternness I could command.

He finally brought the children out (they had gone to sleep in the lodge), and by this time it was nearly midnight.

77

When I saw that he had finally given up and would let me take the children, and knowing that we would be late and that everybody would be disturbed by their return, I did a thing which another might not have done. I turned to Hippy and said, "If you will bring these children to school by sunrise tomorrow I will not take them with me tonight."

He replied, "If you will not whip them I will bring them to school by sunrise tomorrow."

I said, "I shall whip them when they come."

He was deeply troubled, but at last he said, "I will have them there."

With perfect confidence in his word I mounted my horse and we went back to school.

In the morning just as the sun rose Hippy came with the fourteen children. I marched them all up on the porch and got me a whip and prepared to punish them. Hippy again interceded for his little girl and said, "See how innocent she looks! She is already afraid and is beginning to cry."

"I shall whip her all the same," I said, for I knew Hippy had instigated all the trouble. I had now gained my point in every particular and as I passed down the line I simply tapped each child on the shoulder not enough to hurt them, and when the children saw that my whipping was merely a farce, they all began to laugh and even Hippy's grim features changed pleasantly.

Chapter VII

HIPPY GOES INTO

CAPTIVITY AND DIES

OF COURSE, this episode with all its details was soon related in camp. Hippy had again been beaten at his own game, and the Indians made life a burden for Hippy by shouting out "Meokany!" whenever he passed.

The continual dancing and councilling among the Cheyennes caused many people to think they were planning another outbreak. A private soldier one day asked an Indian if they were going on the warpath. He replied, "We may come up to Fort Reno and take the Post."

The soldier seriously replied, "You can't do that, for we will get into the stockade and corral where we would be protected and we could stand you off until help came."

The Cheyenne smiled, "We would not be foolish enough to give you time to get into the corral. We would simply set the haystacks afire some night and when you ran down to put the fire out we would kill you all before you got back."

This was only banter, but it showed that some of the young

fellows thought and talked about how they could take the Post should they attack it, and Hippy's plotting against me was probably in hopes that something might be done that would cause an outbreak. They were tired of the camp life and longed for their buffalo meat and their wild free life. They were like a lot of caged eagles.

They were, in fact, prisoners, not being allowed to hunt buffalo even with a detail of soldiers. They felt the confinement very much, and a certain class of reckless and restless men would rather take the chances of the warpath than remain confined at the agency, pretending to learn the white man's ways. While they rested there in prison others were killing the buffalo in thousands—soon they would all be driven away.

But Hippy's followers gave up all designs upon me. They said, "He is a medicine man and it would be no credit to kill him. He would just as soon die as live."

Hippy soon moved away after this and put up his lodge at Bear Creek—some twelve miles from the agency. I did not know this, and one day while I was out in that neighborhood looking after some cattle I saw some lodges down by the creek and thought I would get down from my horse and rest awhile. I had some suspicion that the Indians had been killing some of the school herd that had strayed out in that neighborhood, and I wished to see what Indians were camped so far away from the main camp, believing that they isolated themselves in that way for no good.

Imagine my surprise to find it Hippy's lodge, and there he sat with the same crowd around him that was with him the night I went after the children.

He greeted me cordially and gave me a comfortable seat and went on relating some jokes which he had in mind. He did not allow my presence to interfere in any way with his stories. After one Indian had related a joke on another, which generally caused them all to laugh very heartily, the proper thing for the victim to do was to rise, shake hands with the joker and try to get even. Finally it came Hippy's turn to tell another joke on some one present, which he did, and the party on whom he told it jumped up and shook hands with him cordially, and then turned and said, "Hippy is getting to be quite a good white man, since the time Meokany threw him off the porch and choked him; and since the time Meokany kicked him out in the yard, and had him put in the guard-house, he has been doing quite well."

Then it was Hippy's turn to shake hands with him and come back at him. Hippy did so, and in reply said, "It is true Meokany and I have had some difficulty, but I don't do like some of the rest of you—steal cattle from his herd, and then accuse him of doing it himself."

I knew the Indian character well enough to know that coming into Hippy's lodge as a passer-by I was safe; otherwise I would have had some uneasiness. An Indian will never take revenge upon a person who comes into his lodge as a friend. Had I met Hippy in the same party out on the prairie when I was alone it might have been different, but in his lodge I was safe. The protection of the two Arapahoe boys on the former occasion arose from the fact I was with them, and that they were in a certain sense, hostages for me and the Arapahoe tribe, with which Cheyennes were at peace. Therefore, Hippy in doing harm to me would be violating a law, which would ever after outlaw him.

It is worth while to note that in my trouble with him, he never took his children from the school and they were obedient and faithful. There was a good heart in the old man —only he could not stand the taunts of his fellows.

Several years after this, Hippy, wishing for some excitement, got up a scheme to kill the agent, John D. Miles. It was during the winter of 1880—the beef issued to the Indians had become poor—but for this the agent was not to blame. He was obliged to receive any beef delivered to him, no matter how bad. If the beef weighed less than a certain amount per head, the agent could make a very large reduction, but could not reject it. The winter was very hard and cattle driven up from Texas reached the agency thin and tough.

Hippy and some of his followers refused to take the beef issued to them, and notified the agent that if he did not get better beef they would kill him. The agent thought nothing of it, supposing that it was an idle threat.

One day my friend, Wolf Robe, came to me and said, "Hippy has got a party organized to kill the agent, and we have had guards standing around the agent's house for several nights to prevent him from going to the agent's house and hauling him out and killing him. We have also kept watch at the agent's office and shadowed him during the day to prevent any of their party from taking his life. Something should be done about it, but I don't want it known that I have informed on them."

I went to the agent and told him that I would watch and see whether this was so or not, and if it was I would report

Courtesy Oklahoma Historical Society

A GROUP AT COLONY

Left to right: George Bent (son of William Bent, founder of
Bent's Fort), Mrs. George Bent, Mrs. Big Knee,
Big Knee, Unknown, John H. Seger, Mr. White (Journalist).

to him. I found that it was as Wolf Robe had told me; Hippy
and a party of young men came to the agency every day with
their weapons in their hands, seeking an opportunity to carry
out their plan.

After I had reported this to the agent, he said, "If you'll
set to work to arrest Hippy and take him to Fort Reno guardhouse you need not attend to any other duty. Go about it in
your own way."

The next day being cold and drizzly I went to the trading
store with my overcoat on, wearing my revolver beneath it.
I had told Wolf Robe that I was going to arrest Hippy, not
supposing he would let the matter be known. I stayed around
the agency trading store all day but Hippy was shy. I concluded I would go to his camp and arrest him. Proceeding to
Wolf Robe's lodge I asked him to show me where Hippy's
lodge was. I told him I was going to arrest him.

He said, "I will go with you, but you better go as an Indian. Put on blanket and moccasins." This I did and Wolf
Robe went with me. He led me to the outskirts of the camp
and pointed out a lodge, which had no light in it. It was about
9 o'clock at night, an hour when all lodges are generally lighted
by an inside fire. When I saw this dark lodge I said to Wolf
Robe, "There is no one at home."

He said, "Let us go up closer—if there is any one there we
can hear them talking."

In creeping towards the lodge we stumbled over a man
lying flat on the ground. Wolf Robe nudged me and pulled
me towards him, and started off away from the lodge. We
were close enough to hear several voices in the lodge talking
very earnestly.

After we had gone some distance from the lodge, Wolf Robe said, "The man we stumbled over was a guard who had been put there to watch, to prevent you from coming to the lodge without due notice. Those talking were Hippy's friends, and are prepared for you, and it will not do for you to try to go into the lodge tonight. If you try it you will surely be killed."

I abandoned the scheme of arresting Hippy that night and the next morning I went to the agency feeling sure Hippy would be there. I watched all day for him and had a team standing in front of the agent's office, ready to whirl him over to the Post. I also had a man picked out to drive the team, and two men were posted in the agent's office to protect him, and to help me manage Hippy in case I grappled with him.

He evidently thought that because I did not come into his lodge that night he had me bluffed, and next day about 4 o'clock he came to the agency. As he entered the store he waggishly stuck his tongue out at me and passed on to the counter, and asked the trader if he had any caps for revolvers. The trader told him that he did have the caps but that he could not sell them to him without an order from the agent.

Hippy recklessly replied, "I wanted them to use in killing the agent." He took out his revolver and showed it and said, "There are six loads in it, and if I can not finish the agent with them, I have a good sharp knife in my belt. I can kill the agent without buying any more caps."

I could see that he was saying this for my benefit. I thought I would shadow him for a while and see if I could determine the members of his party. There were quite a number of In-

dians in the store, but none that I suspected of being in league
with him, so I waited developments.

He finally went out of this trading store and into another,
and I soon followed him. There he met several Indians whom
I suspected. As I came in he showed by his actions that he
knew I was following him. He stayed there until it was almost
sundown and then I concluded I had better arrest him. I knew
the Indians in league with him and against whom I would
have to guard myself. Sitting on the counter was a cowboy,
named Ben Good. Ben was counted one of the best revolver
shots in the country, and had the name of having killed his
man, and it was understood that he was "hiding out" at this
time, although the people at Darlington were not the ones
that wanted him. I told Ben that I was going to arrest Hippy
and pointed out three Indians whom I believed would interfere in the matter. I said, "Will you take your pistol and stand
them off while I am arresting Hippy?"

"Go ahead," said he, "I'll shoot the first one that interferes
with you."

Ben always had a six-shooter in his belt and while I was
talking with him he began fingering it with his right hand
and Hippy who was watching me all the time I was talking
with him became uneasy. He rose and went out of the store
and as I stepped to the door after him I saw him going around
the corner of the agency commissary leading to the agent's
office. As soon as he turned the corner I ran after him, thinking
I would get to the corner of the commissary about the time
that he had started up the stairs leading to the office, but
when I came running up, Hippy, to my surprise, had antici-

pated that I would follow him and was crouching behind the corner of the building.

Quick as a flash I looked the other way and started towards my own home. After I had walked several rods I glanced over my shoulder and saw Hippy mounting the stairs. As soon as he passed into the door I darted after him, jerking away my overcoat as I ran. When Hippy entered the office he found several friendly Indians sitting there. They, knowing there would be trouble, got up and rushed out. Just as they came to the door they saw me throw off my overcoat. As I entered Hippy was leaning over the railing talking to a clerk.

Before he could turn I seized him around the body holding his arms pressed tight to his sides. He tried to get a hold of his revolver or knife, but I held him fast and the clerk jumped over the railing and snapped a pair of handcuffs on him. Johnny Murphy came out of the agent's office, and carrying Hippy we started down the stairs as fast as we could go. On the way down he started to give a yell, probably to some of his followers, when Covington undertook to cram a handkerchief in his mouth. In trying to do so, he got his fingers in our prisoner's mouth, which caused the clerk to do the yelling.

Seizing Hippy's throat I made him let go of the finger. I kept my hand on his throat thereafter, to prevent him from whooping. We put him into the wagon and soon had the horses on the keen jump for the Post. When we reached there, we took Hippy to the guardhouse and with deep breaths of relief left him in charge of the guard.

In the meantime Hippy's followers, three of them, learned that he had been taken and felt some uneasiness about themselves, and as Covington, Murphy, and myself were returning to the agency in the wagon, we saw the three Indians coming towards us. But when we got closer to them we saw that they were looking pleasant and very good-natured, and when we got up to them, they signaled for us to stop and came up into the wagon and hugged each one of us.

We saw that they were disposed to be friendly and not to resent Hippy's capture. A few days later Hippy was sent to Fort Smith as a prisoner. During the two years of his stay Hippy worked on the rockpile with other prisoners. He got into difficulty one day with another prisoner who was working with him and was knocked down. He fell upon the pile of rock, injuring his old wound, and was so crippled that he was never able to walk again. The authorities then sent him back to Darlington.

A short time after he returned I visited a Sun Dance which the Indians were holding at the time. They were camped as they always were on such occasions in the shape of a horseshoe. I was going around this circle visiting old friends and stopping at each lodge as I passed to have a few words with each family. All at once with deep surprise I recognized Hippy lying helpless on a cot in a lodge with the side raised. Not considering him a special friend I was about to pass by without noticing him, when he called to me, "What are you afraid of? I won't hurt you if you come in here."

I then turned into the lodge and said, "I am not afraid of you, Hippy, but I did not care to speak to you."

"You are afraid of me, that is the reason you did not want to come in. I have no gun, only this knife to fight with." Thereupon he pulled a knife out from under his pillow and showed it to me. "I want you to sit down here and listen to what I have to say."

He then recounted his experience at Fort Smith and all the incidents of his return, and when he was through I left him and we shook hands.

I saw him again a few years afterwards at Darlington. He was lying in his wagon on a mattress, and again he called me up to him. He said, "I want to shake hands with you again. Most of the white people that have come to the agency to work with the Indians have left—they come and go—these white people—but you are the only one who stays with us. It seems good to see you again, for I have known you a long time. I shall not live much longer, and I wanted to have a few words with you, and shake your hand again before I die."

A short time after this Hippy died, and as he lay upon his death bed, he called his children around him, and gave them his last message. "My children, when you have little ones to send to school, take them to Meokany; he is a good man and strong medicine." Then the indomitable soul of this strange man failed him and he died.

Chapter VIII

I FOUND THE
INDIAN SCHOOL AND
TOWN OF COLONY

For two years I was continually fencing for cattle men, during which time I built 300 miles of fence.

The terms of lease of the cattle men were that they should hire Indians to help them with their cattle.

The excuse the cattle men had for not doing this at first was that the Indian did not know how to hold cattle on open range, and it would be all right after they got the pastures fenced—then the Indians could ride the fenced land and tend the round-ups and help in branding.

As the fence was not done for two years, there was very little Indian help used in handling cattle. I used them all the time in my fence work and found them the best help I could get. I insisted on the cattle men hiring them, especially to ride the fence lines and keep the fence in repair.

They always had some excuse for not doing so.

I took the contract of keeping the fence on a string of about 50 miles. I hired two Indians to do the work.

They did this work satisfactorily until the cattle men left the country. When they did, the Indians hired out to help drive cattle on the trail. The boss who had charge of them said they were among his best hands.

This shows what might have been done had the cattle men complied strictly with this part of the contract. Had they done so it is very likely the lease would not have been cancelled within two years from the time it was made, as was done.

Most of the men who held cattle in the Cheyenne and Arapahoe country were Texas men who were prejudiced against the Indians. They did not understand the Indians and for this reason it was not very easy for the Indians to understand them.

After the fence was built on the south side of the leased lands, the Kiowas made no further trouble except to go up into the pastures and occasionally steal a beef. They used to manage this very skillfully. They would go and visit the ranches, where the men were scattered, and would get acquainted with every man and learn his habits, and where each man would be a certain time of the day. Then they would visit that ranch in a sufficient number so that they could have some man shadow each person to tell where they were, and could notice if any of the cowboys were liable to run on to them while they were butchering the beef.

Then a small party would start off and go out to the creek to kill a beef while their companions were watching the cow men in order to give the signal in case they were liable to be discovered.

The cattle men would frequently find where the beef had been killed and thought it very strange they could not discover the one who did it. Finally after some time they got acquainted with the method the Kiowas used, and then when a party of Indians came to the headquarters ranch of the A. V. Ranch the boss concluded they had come to get a beef as usual. So he sent a party of men to watch where the party would kill the beef. The Kiowas started off as though going home. After the Indians had killed the beef, the cowboys suddenly came upon them skinning it. This was too much for the Texas cowboys and they fired a volley at the Indians, wounding one of them.

After they saw what they had done, Ragner and the cowboys became very much excited and rode to my ranch about fifteen miles away. Ragner told me what they had done and advised me to take my family and flee to Darlington or as near the agency as possible. As for himself he was going to Ft. Reno. He said no doubt when the news reached the Kiowas that one of their party had been hit, a war party would visit the locality as soon as possible.

He said he had instructed his men all to go to the ranch and collect everything and defend themselves. He would report the matter at Ft. Reno and he hoped they would send some troops out.

I told him I would pay no attention to it until I saw some indication that there was danger, so he left. I did not hear any more of this until some years later.

The lease the cattle men had with the Indians allowed the Indians to occupy any part of the leased ground they wished and to graze their ponies upon it—to have the same freedom to roam over it that they would have had if the cattlemen had not had it leased.

When the Indians undertook to do this, in a great many instances many of the cattle men were suspicious of the Indians. They thought the Indians were there to steal cattle and were afraid they would set the grass afire. They were anxious to have them ordered into the agency, and sometimes, there is no doubt, the cattlemen sent in false reports to the agent in order to get the agent to order the Indians into Darlington.

This, of course, made some dissatisfaction among the Indians.

I stood good for the conduct of the Indians working for me, and when a report came to me of anything detrimental to their behavior I investigated it and in every instance found that the charge against the Indian was false. The average cowboy did not want to see the Indian succeed as a cowboy, as he knew his chance for employment would be that much lessened, so the features most beneficial to the Indian in the lease were not carried out.

Then, as was proposed in the lease, that part of the money derived from leasing the land should be invested in cattle for the Indians, to be held and allowed to increase until they would stock the range with cattle was also disregarded. I think the traders had a great deal to do with this. The money the Indians received for the lease was about $60,000.00 per year. Afterwards part of their grazing land was leased, so altogether they received $100,000.00 a year.

A delegation of chiefs visited Washington for the purpose of getting all the money paid to them instead of half of it being invested in cattle. They succeeded in getting this change made, so that the most beneficial clauses of the lease were now done away with, and it simply gave the Indians $100,000.00 a year to spend, in two semi-annual payments.

Most of the Indians had moved in around Darlington and it was the policy of the agent to open up small farms, ten acres and upwards, which he claimed a farmer could supervise and thus teach them a great deal better than if they were scattered over the reservation.

This part of it, no doubt, was true, and some of the Indians made very good progress in farming small patches of ground and they raised a good deal of corn, and had a ready market among the cow men at from fifty cents to $1.00 per bushel.

They hauled freight from Caldwell, Kansas, 100 miles distant, for which they received $1.00 per 100 for hauling.

This furnished those who wanted to work, quite an income; the Indians were well satisfied with these conditions.

While they were confined to the land in the immediate vicinity of the agency, the grass became very scant for their ponies. When they wished to go out over the reservation for the purpose of grazing their ponies, they were always troubled by cattle men, and false reports would come to Darlington from the cattle men. The most progressive Indians, those who wanted to do something, were very dissatisfied with this arrangement. There were quite a number who settled down at the agency, putting in some of their time in gambling and loafing around the trading store. Another class who wished to be moving around were very much dissatisfied with the conditions.

Certain squaw-men who wished to make use of the Indian

reservation had married into the tribe, expecting in this way to get a good cattle range, and were very much dissatisfied with the leasing of all this land. There was soon pressure brought to bear upon the government to have the lease cancelled. In the change of administration (1884) after President Cleveland was inaugurated, the parties opposing the lease of the land made an effort to have it cancelled.

Agent Dire, who succeeded John D. Miles as agent, was a new man among the Indians. He did not understand them overly well. He no doubt was appointed through the influence of the cattle men, thinking he would probably cater to their wishes. Through his action he furnished the opportune time for those who were opposing the lease to succeed in their efforts in getting it cancelled.

As was before stated some of the Indians were complaining of their treatment by the cattle men and would not always come into Darlington when the agent ordered them to do so. Agent Dire wishing to be obeyed promptly by the Indians advised that there should be a larger number of soldiers sent to Ft. Reno, as at the time there was a very small garrison. He thought that if the government would send quite a number of troops it would awe the Indians into humble obedience.

In order to make a sufficient reason for the government to send these troops, he sent in a very alarming report of the unsettled condition of the Indians and the possibility of their going on the warpath unless they were checked. At this time I visited Darlington from my home at Pond Creek. As I passed through Ft. Reno, the commanding officer met me. He asked me what I thought of the probability of the Indians going on the warpath. I told him I did not think there was any probability of their doing so.

He said the people at Darlington were very much alarmed and the agent had reported that there was danger of an outbreak, and recommended increasing the garrison at Ft. Reno.

I told him I had left my family thirty miles away without any precaution and I had come into Darlington without any weapons of any kind with me. I felt no uneasiness whatever, that I was going to Darlington, where I would meet Indians whom I knew well, I would find out from them their feelings towards the agency and white people. I would know whether there was any danger of an outbreak.

I went to Darlington and found that the employees had been changed with the exception of two or three, owing to the change of agents, and those I knew were entirely unacquainted with the Indians and did not understand their movements and their actions in the least.

As I was standing in front of the trader's store I saw a body of about thirty young Indians riding into the agency on horseback. As they entered the agency they fired a volley into the air. I saw the agency employees looked very much frightened. The agency physician, who was standing near me, fairly trembled, and said, "See those blood-thirsty villains! I believe they are going to attack the agency."

I told him he need not be alarmed. They were evidently getting up a Sun Dance and those were the Dog Soldiers who were riding around giving notice to the Indians to move together to the dance.

He said, "Why do they carry their guns then, and fire them while coming into the agency?"

I told him that was the signal. A party of Indians who come into another camp of Indians fire all their guns to let the camp know they are coming with empty guns, which was a sign of friendship. They did so at the agency in compliance with this custom.

I said, "If they were warlike each would reserve his ammunition, instead of wasting it by firing it into the air." In the past all ammunition was very scarce among the Indians and they never fired it without some motive for doing so.

As the Dog Soldiers came closer the doctor saw that their faces were painted. They were dressed in full Indian costume, and he was satisfied they were preparing for an outbreak.

Wolf Robe being in the crowd saw me, rode out of the crowd and motioned for me to come out to where he was. I went out and shook hands with him. I asked him what was going on. They were getting up a Sun Dance. I told him then the agency employees were very much alarmed, thinking the Indians were going on the warpath.

Wolf Robe commenced to laugh very heartily to think they were afraid, and it amused him very much. I spoke in a low voice to Wolf Robe, and asked him to tell me the truth, whether the Indians were liable to go on the warpath. "You know my family is unprotected and a long way from here."

Wolf Robe broke out in a laugh and asked me if I had gone crazy. He said he believed I was about to become a big fool.

I insisted that he tell me the truth about it, and he saw I was earnest in my inquiry, and so he became sober himself and said, "No." He said there was no danger whatever. After the war of 1874 the Indians fully decided that they could not fight with the white people, he said, so they decided to live in peace with them ever afterwards.

He said, "This you can see from the fact that we have at

this time about 250 of the Cheyenne and Arapahoe children in Eastern schools. We have put them in the hands of white men. Do you think we would put them in the hands of our enemies? We believe the white men are our friends. We are going to live in peace with them; therefore, as a pledge to the friendship, we have put our children in their hands. They are just the same as prisoners, should we commit any depredation or massacre. We do not know but what the white people would like to take revenge on our children. It would be like murdering our own children.

"These white people here do not understand us. They are frightened at what we do and we enjoy seeing their uneasiness."

I was thoroughly convinced in my own mind, although I had no fears previous to this, yet I took this course with Wolf Robe in order to satisfy the commanding officer. Wolf Robe's version of the case I thought sufficient to convince any reasonable person there was no danger.

Those who wished to have the lease cancelled took the opportunity of this state of affairs to work against the lease. General Sheridan was sent to Darlington to look over the situation and to take the matter in hand and to see if there was any danger of an uprising, and if so, to take steps to prevent it.

When General Sheridan got to Darlington he saw that the whole matter had been brought about by the cattle men out of the country, and he put military men in charge of the agency.

Ever since the military had occupied Ft. Reno there had been some dissatisfaction on the part of the military in being called upon to carry out plans and enforce the orders of a

97

civilian agent, as a colonel or captain or soldiers did not like to take orders from a citizen. They felt the military should have charge of the Indians as long as they had to be on the ground and maintain order and look after the safety of the people in the country.

This furnished an opportunity and General Sheridan made use of it. President Cleveland notified Agent Dire that his resignation would be expected. This was not done, however, until an inspector was sent out and looked into affairs generally.

Agent Dire was allowed to send in his resignation and Capt. Jesse Lee was requested by President Cleveland to act as agent to the Cheyennes and Arapahoes.

This change of affairs took the cattle men by surprise and put them in a very bad condition, as the order for the lease to be cancelled was promulgated at once and they were only given forty days to move the cattle out of the country.

They had brought large herds of cattle from Texas, driven them through and put them on this ranch. They had just fairly got their branding pens and corrals completed and had comfortable buildings put up for their men. In some instances they had erected frame houses and had subdivided their range into pastures suitable for their business as they expected the lease to last ten years. To be obliged to move out in forty days was a great calamity.

They sent a delegation to Washington to enter protest. The Board of Trade of Kansas City sent a delegation and President Cleveland gave them hearing. After they had made their plea before him for an extension of time they offered to pay their lease six months in advance if they were allowed to

The Schoolboy, before Enrollment

Another Schoolboy, after Graduation

remain until the Spring. They told him they would go in strict accordance to his orders—but that it would annihilate $6,000,-000.00, which would leave many of the cattle companies, if not all of them, bankrupt.

President Cleveland replied, "Gentlemen, you are wasting much time in coming here to protest against the carrying out of this order. You had better be at home getting your cattle off the reservation."

The work commenced at once of moving the cattle out. The range was very scarce and they were put to a great deal of trouble to find any place where they could raise their cattle, the majority of them—having been driven from Texas—were too poor to put upon the market.

The best information I could get, nearly every cattle company went bankrupt. The hundreds of miles of fence that had been built had to be taken down, and the wire rolled up and disposed of.

I being located in the leased ground came under the order of the cattle men, as I had a horse ranch, and I prepared to leave. I had spent a great deal of money fitting it up, and found to leave so abruptly would leave me about the same as it did the cattle men. Horses as well as cattle were a drug on the market.

I determined to leave the Indian country, where I had spent about twenty years of the best of my life, and go where I could have the advantage of civilization and put my children in school. Kansas being the nearest point where I could stop outside of the Indian country, I made arrangements to move to that state.

When Capt. Lee came to Darlington and looked around

over the situation he found the government rations had been cut down somewhat owing to the fact that the Indians were getting so much money paid them for the lease of their lands. Now, as this lease money would be cut off, he saw the Indians would be left really destitute.

The War Department came to the rescue by hiring one hundred Indian scouts at $25.00 per month and clothing, who were to be made use of in helping to get the cattle men out of the country and to protect old Oklahoma from the boomer element trying to settle in the country contrary to law.

These scouts were taken from different families so that nearly every family was represented in the scout service, therefore receiving more revenue in this way.

Capt. Lee found there was a large camp of Indians settled in the immediate vicinity of the agency. When he talked with them they did not seem to have any aim in life, beyond gambling, dancing, and spending their time in idleness.

When the grass payment was made these Indians had been accustomed to gambling and had become experts, and no doubt got more than their legitimate share of lease money.

After the money was spent and the Indians had no more money to gamble with, then they would run in debt towards the next payment. In this way they were eeking out an existence.

Capt. Lee went about energetically to induce the Indians to commence farming and do work. He found when he talked to these Indians they had no interest whatever for anything like work. There was another class among the Cheyennes and Arapahoes who were willing to farm or do anything to earn a living. They said owing to this large camp at Darlington, they did not have much ambition. When they earned a dollar these lazy, gambling Indians would be ready to help them eat it up. They said when they hauled a load of freight from Caldwell these Indians were always sitting around the traders' stores and knew when they would get this money, and would follow them and help them eat the provisions they bought with their money. They said if they raised a crop of corn these Indians would help them eat it up.

This feature of the agency bothered the captain a great deal and while talking over the matter in the trading store one day, he said, "If I could take these Indians that are camped around the agency here, what I call coffee-coolers, or Indians who do nothing, if I could move them fifty miles from the agency and order them there I could take the rest of the Indians and get them to farming and industry and make a rapid advancement."

After saying this he returned to the crowd and said, "Do you suppose such a thing could be done as moving these Indians so far from the agency and keeping them there?"

John Murphy, who was present, and a man who had been at Darlington ever since the agency first started said, "Captain, if there is anybody that could do this it is John H. Seger."

He told of some of the things I had accomplished with the Indians in the way of carrying mail, having them cut cord wood and make brick; also such industries as they had been engaged in under my direction.

Capt. Lee said, "Where is this Seger?"

Murphy said, "He will be coming to the agency in a few days on his way to Kansas."

Lee said, "Bring him to my office when he comes through. I want to talk with him."

When I came to Darlington on my way to Kansas I met John Murphy, and he said, "Seger, Capt. Lee wants to see you up in his office."

I went with him to the agent's office and Murphy introduced me to the captain.

The captain began at once stating the case to me in regard to these non-progressive Indians. He said, "Do you think they could be moved out fifty miles from the agency and kept there?"

I said, "Captain, I could take them Indians and move about fifty miles from the agency and keep them there, but I don't intend to do it. I am leaving the Indian country for good. I have spent the best part of my life here in trying to help these Indians and I have not accomplished much for the Indians, as far as I can see. I have been under many privations on account of being among them and now I am going to a white man's country where I can educate my children and take a little of the comforts of life as I go along."

Captain Lee then said I ought not to do this; my experience among these people was invaluable in the line of civilizing them, as it would take any other person a long time to get the experience I had and be in a position to do what I could accomplish with them.

I told him as far as the position was concerned or the salary connected with it, I would not give the matter a moment's thought. If I could take up some work among these Indians and carry it through to a successful ending and feel that I had accomplished some good work that I might consider as a life work, something I could look back to in my old age I might be induced to undertake it. I told him I had learned this: no one, no matter how experienced, could civilize these Indians in three or four years. The matter would be a life work for any one.

He said, of course, as agent he could not insure any position to me for any length of time. He believed as long as he was agent he could keep me in a position which he recommended, but further than that he could make no promises.

I told him as far as that was concerned I had never asked to be appointed in the Indian service. I had never had any influence to keep me there, and I was willing to take the chance of holding my position if I was once put into it. I did not speak of the matter of being retained on account of wanting to hold my job, but simply wished to explain that a person could not get satisfactory results in a very short period of Indian service.

After talking awhile I finally told him if I succeeded in locating my family comfortably in some town in Kansas, where my children would have good school advantages, I would return without my family and would undertake to move those Indians away from Darlington, provided he got authority from the Indian office to have them moved away.

He told me to return as soon as I could. He would provide me with temporary employment until he could get the proper authority for moving the Indians away from the agency.

I took my family to Caldwell, Kansas, where I bought a small house and settled my family comfortably. In a short time I was back in Darlington ready to go into the Indian service. It was four months from that time before Capt. Lee could get the necessary authority to move the Indians. He had to work very hard to show the department the need of doing so. He had to solicit the aid of inspectors or any person of influence whom he might meet and could interest in the plan. In the meantime he wished to let a contract for saw logs with the agency sawmill. I told him I would bid upon this contract, agreeing to do all the work with Indian labor and Indian teams.

This pleased him very much. As I was familiar with logging and knew where the timber was along the North Fork, I had the lowest bid and was awarded the contract. This work commenced in the winter, when the Indians' teams were poor in flesh and at a time when Indians are less willing to work than at any other season of the year, as there was considerable bad weather.

I succeeded in getting the Indians to do this work in a creditable manner and to the satisfaction of the agent. These were the only Indians that were doing work of any consequence at that time.

The agent had told me the position he expected to give me was one classed as position of agency farmer, with a salary of $75.00 a month. This position he said he had not asked the government to fill with the exception of having me appointed to the place when the necessary authority was granted for moving the Indians.

Finally the authority came for the Indians to be moved and an appropriation for doing some breaking and fencing; also other work necessary to establish the Colony. About the time this authority came the agent was notified that the position he had been saving for me was filled by an opponent.

The person came on to take the place. He was an old gentleman about 76 years old, who had epileptic fits. He had been Indian agent sometime in the past, and when he was agent he had done favor to some person who was now holding a high position at Washington. Through him he got this appointment. Capt. Lee was almost frantic when he saw this man could not do the work he had planned to have done. He came to me and said, "Seger, I do not know what to do."

After he related the condition he said, "If I just had a little time to lay the matter before the department I believe I could get this matter changed and could get the position for you alright."

He said, "I would not send this man five miles from Darlington, as it would be cruel to send an old gentleman in his condition so far away."

He said, "It is already time the Indians were moving out to get ready for farming, and should I delay the matter longer it will be too late to accomplish much this year in farming."

He said, "I got the authority for doing this fencing and work, and the work ought to be going on at once."

I asked the Captain what terms the appropriation was made in. He said it was made in view of his letting the contract to some one to do the work. I told him I would take the contract of doing that work. At the same time I would move the Indians fifty miles from Darlington. I would pay my own expenses, wages, and do all the work with the Indians while filling the contract.

He said if I could do this he thought in a short time he would get matters shaped so he could put me on a salary as he first intended to do.

I went to work at once to get up a party to move to Cobb Creek and Washita, a point where I had been living while running my horse ranch and building a fence for the cattle company.

I spent some time in looking up a location when I settled there. I was satisfied this place was the best one to move the Indians to.

I went to camp and invited some of the head men to meet me at Capt. Lee's office at night, where we would talk over the plan in regard to their welfare.

The Indians were on hand. We began to explain the project to them. They at first did not think favorably of it, as they saw so many objections. I knew their rations did not furnish them enough for them to live on—when they were out far from the agency they might starve before they could get their rations, they said.

They said they were drawing rations once a week and they had enough to live on about four days and three days they could fast and drink water, but if they went so far from the agency they would have to draw their rations for a longer period of time and they would probably eat them up in nearly half the time they were to last, and there would be no other Indians near whom they might visit and eat with. They could see no way how they could bridge over that time.

I told them I would go with them—would live with them and fare as they fared. If they starved I would starve with them.

The first ones who gave their names as being willing to join the party and move to Washita were sixteen of my old school children who had been to school when I was super-intendent in 1875.

They had now grown up and were married and had families. Then came the immediate relations and friends of these children and some of the old Indians who had been the first ones to put their children in my school when I was superintendent and had given me loyal support.

I soon had a party of 120 Arapahoes on the road.

Chapter IX

THE COMING OF

MY FAMILY

WHEN I MOVED out to Colony I fully expected to leave my family in Caldwell, Kansas, where my children could go to school. My plan was to live in the lodges of my colonists until I could get some few of them to build houses; then I expected to go from house to house instructing them in the use of white men's furniture, etc. But the death of my little boy decided my wife's plans. She resolved to come where I was regardless of all privations and hardships.

So in June of the first year of my Colony she and the children came out. I had no house for her, only the cabin I had built while working for the cattlemen, and some one had stolen the windows and floors and doors of this.

Captain Lee supplied me with flooring, doors and windows, and my family moved in. We lived in these two dirt-roof cabins until 1891 with no other shelter provided by the government.

My district now extended over an area of 25 by 40 miles,

108

and as I was away from home most of the time my wife and children had to remain at the headquarters with no white neighbors nearer than Darlington. But my children had been born among the Indians and looked upon these folks the same as other folks. The Indian women were very kind and neighborly, and often touched our hearts by their good will.

When our supplies were exhausted I had to leave my family and go to Darlington to secure provisions. Sometimes I was gone as long as two weeks, for the Canadian River is a treacherous stream and was more than likely to rise immediately after I had crossed leaving me in great anxiety on the wrong side.

I always put off these trips until going was absolutely necessary. On several occasions had it not been for the kindly help of the Indians, my family would have suffered for the want of food.

On one occasion I was on my way home and had got as far as the Canadian River. The river was out of its banks and quite impassable. There was nothing to do but stay on the bank and wait for it to go down, which I did very unwillingly, for I knew that provisions were scarce in the Seger cabin.

After I had been there two or three days I saw a wagon drive up on the opposite side of the river, and soon two Indians took the harness off of the horses and mounted preparatory to swimming across to my side of the river.

I hastened to meet them and inquire how things were going. It had been some ten days since I left home and I was very glad to learn that all was well.

The Indians remarked: "As long as our people have something to eat your family will not go hungry." They added:

"We are getting short of supplies ourselves and we are going to the agency to get supplies."

As they could not get their wagons across they had concluded to swim across with their horses and ride into the agency and get some supplies and come back and swim across the river with it.

It was just night when they came across and they rode on to Darlington about twenty miles distant. They were back again by the next evening with supplies of baking powder, bacon, and lard, resolute to cross.

The river was still very high, but they decided to take a few of the supplies and go across and hurry home and report the conditions to my people and to their people.

Each man tied a piece of bacon behind his saddle, and each took a can of lard in his hand, while he held the reins in the other. I want to say that it took courage to enter that flood. When they had gotten about half across the river they struck a quick-sandy bar and their horses began to plunge furiously to keep from sinking. This plunging jerked the cans of lard out of their hands, but they sprang off their horses and swam after the cans of lard and baking powder.

This was not all their discouragements. Before starting they had loosened the girths of their saddles in order to give their horses more breathing space and the jumping and plunging of the horses caused their saddles to slip off over the cruppers.

Jock Bull Bear, seeing his saddle was floating away, made a dash for the saddle and caught it. He then had a can of lard in one hand and the saddle in the other, but he got back to where he started.

As the saddle weighed about thirty-five pounds I never could see how he accomplished this tremendous feat. I have never seen a braver fight.

The horses swam across to the west side where the wagons were. Both of the Indians now came back to where I was and remained over night. Jock took no thought of the danger he had been in, but regretted the loss of the can of lard.

The river went down some that night so we concluded to try and cross the river. I told them I would try it with them this time. "I will pack the horses with such supplies as I can. If we reach the other side I will take my team and go on, leaving my wagon for you to bring when you can."

I had with me two mules and one horse. One of the mules could not be ridden or packed, so the two brave fellows swam across and brought their ponies over. I then packed one of the mules with flour and bacon and such supplies and also the extra horse I had with me.

I put both the harnesses on the mule that could not be ridden. Knowing he would follow his mate, I tied a line in the hame ring and took hold of the line and told the Indians to go ahead and lead the pack horses and the mule would follow. "I will hang onto this line and let him tow me across," said I. This amused them very much and we started.

We got on very well, although the water was still nearly half a mile wide from bank to bank. I must confess I felt lonesome while hanging to that line with a mule swimming ahead of me and one-quarter of a mile of water on each side of me, and my respect for Jock and his companion went up several notches further.

When we reached the center of the river we struck a sand

bar which barely showed itself above the water. We then discovered that one of the packs had turned on the side of the horse and should be straightened at once.

The bar was a perfect quicksand, neither horse nor man could stand a minute without sinking. I turned my mule loose and grabbing the pack held it up, telling the Indians to lead the horse up and down the bar until I adjusted the pack-saddle.

They did so and when I had the pack in place they struck out at once to cross the other channel.

The mule that had towed me thus far had been following up and down with the crowd, but when the Indians started out with the pack-animal, he very knowingly struck out a little ahead. I was taken by surprise and he was out of my reach before I could grab the lines. This left me on the quicksand bar in the midst of a half-mile of very red and angry water. There was nothing to do but keep walking and watch the scenery. The farther the boys got toward home the lonesomer it got for me. I kept pacing steadily up and down the bar, knowing that when Jock landed he'd see my need of him. As soon as he got well across Jock turned his packhorse loose and turned back to my rescue.

When I saw him coming I waded out into running water. As he passed me he shouted: "When I pass you again, jump on my horse." I said, "The pony can't carry us." Jock answered, "When he can't I will jump off."

When the pony passed me I made a spring and jumped on behind and down sank the pony till nothing could be seen of us, except our heads and the pony's nose and ears sticking above the water.

We were borne swiftly down with the current but the pony struck bottom at last and Jock jumped off shouting: "Take care of yourself—ride the pony out." The pony was very tired but he crawled up the bank to safety.

I soon had my team hitched and with two pack-loads of supplies set out for home—while Jock and the other Indian returned to take care of the wagon that was on the East side of the river and bring it on later, when the water went down. This incident illustrates the fearlessness and the tenacity of purpose of my red friends.

When I reached home I found my wife and family all well. My wife told me that several of the Indians came clear from the Washita day after day to see if everything was all right at the headquarter ranch. One of these was Big Nose.

When I met the old man I told him I deeply appreciated his kindness toward my family.

He replied: "I never went to bed at night until I had walked all about your house to see that everything was safe."

I was forced to go to Darlington on another occasion in mid-winter. A very bad blizzard came up, which made traveling impossible and kept me at the agency. As before, the Canadian River was the principal barrier to my going home.

Finally, after the storm had subsided, although it was very cold and the weather was not yet settled, I started—for I feared my family would suffer during the blizzard. My wife was alone with only two boys of ten and twelve years old to assist her.

Creeping Bear, a very bright and rather waggish Arapahoe Indian was with me. We reached the Canadian River about sundown. It was frozen over and we thought we could cross on the ice.

We got along very well until we reached the deep water in the main channel. There the ice was smooth, and the mules not being shod fell, and their fall broke the ice and let them in while the wagon dropped with a thud to the bottom.

The water was about three and a half feet deep and running very swiftly. The ice in front of the mules was about breast high. The wheels sank into the quicksand a little so that the water was almost to the top of the wagon box, and my supplies were in danger.

Creeping Bear did not hesitate. He sprang into the water where he was most needed, went to the heads of the mules and held them from plunging—up to his breast in the icy flood.

Reaching down into the water I unhooked the traces. As soon as the mules were freed from the wagon and the lines unbuckled, Creeping Bear climbed upon the ice and succeeded in getting the mules upon the ice again.

Making them fast Creeping Bear returned and we soon threw the load back on the ice behind the wagon and got it out of the water. The question then was how to get the wagon out of the water, but both of us by this time were thoroughly wet and our clothing was coated with ice. An Indian woman was coming down to the river for water. Creeping Bear succeeded in shouting to her and signalled her to tell the men of her camp to come to our aid. She ran back to camp and in a short time a dozen men surrounded us, ready to do anything in their power. With their help we lifted the wagon out and put it on the ice, and carried our supplies across and loaded them in the wagon again. The mules were covered with ice and our clothes were frozen stiff. We were in a pitiable condition, but Creeping Bear did not lose heart.

COLONY MISSION ON THE TRAIL, 1900

Seated, left to right: Rev. Mr. Walter C. Roe (Indian name, "Iron Eyes"), Mrs. Roe, and Rev. Mr. F. H. Wright, D.D.

A mile or two up the river lived a Mexican, married to an Indian woman. I knew if I could reach that place I could get by a fire.

I told Creeping Bear I was going up there and stay that night.

He said: "I would like to go back to the camp and dry myself there."

I told him to go and I drove on. I found the Mexican at home with a good fire in his fireplace. I soon had my team turned out and in shelter. I went in to the fire and dried my clothing and stayed all night. The next morning the sun came out—the weather was considerably moderated, and I reached home without further mishap.

I inquired at once of my wife how she got on in my absence. She said on the morning the blizzard struck them the air was so full of frost and snow that she could not see ten feet ahead of her and she was in distress about her supply of wood and water. She expected to have a very hard time indeed and was getting ready to sally out after wood when old Two Babies, one of the laziest Indians in the colony, came in.

After looking around he picked up the axe and went out and soon brought in a big armful of wood. He worked away until he had stacked up a good supply. He then took the water buckets and went to the spring and filled them with water. He then left without saying a word.

"He kept us in wood and water until the storm was over," my wife said. "I don't know what we would have done without him."

I made it a point when I met Two Babies to thank him for his good heart.

115

He replied: "You are under no obligation to me. What I have done I did for my own comfort and satisfaction. You see when I got up in my lodge and sat before the warm fire I commenced to think about the two little boys who would have to go out in that cold wind and chop wood and carry water. I felt very uncomfortable and could not get my mind off of them. It was in order to satisfy myself I went up and got the wood and water for them. When I returned I could enjoy my own warm lodge."

This was a delicate way of making me feel free of obligations to him for an act he had done through entire goodness of heart.

As my family was fifty-five miles from any white settlement, Darlington being the nearest, we were also that far from a physician or any white woman's care in case of sickness. My eldest daughter became very ill with fever. We had no medicine whatever to keep down the fever, and my wife and I had to sit by her bedside day and night. The Indians offered their assistance and stood ready to help us. But without medicine we could not arrest the disease.

I made it known that I would like to send to the agency physician for medicine. I had no sooner made this want known than War Path stepped up and said: "I will go."

"Very well, War Path," said I. "I will write a letter at once." He started off on the run, saddled his horse and was ready to start by the time the letter was written. He started about nine in the morning. Before daylight the next morning he had returned with the medicine, having ridden one hundred and ten miles in less than twenty-four hours. My heart was big with gratitude toward him but he took the whole trip as quickly as if it had been a trip to the Washita.

I asked him how he succeeded in making such wonderfully quick time.

He replied: "Whenever I struck an Indian camp or met an Indian on horseback I changed horses. I have had several horses since I started from Darlington."

With the help of the medicine we checked the fever. Our daughter's life was saved by the splendid and generous courage of this young red man. Even now I can hardly recall that anxious time and War Path's wonderful ride without a glow at my heart and tears in my eyes.

For several days my daughter had been unable to eat any food whatever and the red people seemed very solicitous about her on this account. One day some women came with a few ripe mulberries which they had picked. "Give them to your daughter; they are good," they said.

Strange to say she ate them and relished them very much.

This pleased them and they soon appeared again with more berries and from that time on seemed to vie with each other doing for us.

All through this sickness my wife was not able to attend anything about the house and one day Eating Woman and Star Woman came and asked permission to do our washing and to clean up the house. My wife was surprised at their doing this as these two women had always held themselves aloof and had not seemed very friendly. They had never visited at our house, although my daughter frequently visited them at camp.

They took hold at once, did the washing and cleaned up

the house, putting everything in order—then went home not waiting for thanks or any recognition for doing so.

At one time during my daughter's illness we had given up all hopes of her recovery and my wife and I began to counsel how we should bury her and where we should make her grave. We had no coffin or lumber to make one or anything to give her a civilized burial, and no one to assist in any way but the Indians. When my daughter recovered, the Indians all expressed much pleasure and in many ways showed how deeply they had sympathized with us all through our trouble. There are a hundred things I might mention—little things which they did. I must tell one more.

One time when I was gone for supplies, my family became quite destitute. It happened that the wife of Wautan, a very nice woman, was at my house helping my wife with her washing and house-cleaning.

When it came dinner time my wife, as usual, asked her to sit up and eat with her, apologizing meanwhile by saying, "I have no sugar to put in your coffee and will not have till Mr. Seger returns from Darlington."

Wautan's wife said: "I have some sugar at my camp. After dinner I will take your little girl home with me and I will divide with you."

When dinner was over with, she took our little girl with her. When she returned she told her mother that Mrs. Wautan had brought out a little sack of sugar and held it in her hand and looked at it. Then drawing a line with her finger through the exact center she put half of it out on a cloth.

While she was doing so Mrs. Creeping Bear came out of another lodge and said: "What are you doing?"

Mrs. Wautan said: "Mrs. Seger has no sugar and I am giving her half of mine."

After the division was made, Mrs. Creeping Bear remarked: "That's such a little bit of sugar—I will give her part of mine."

She had only a little but she divided it and added half of it.

This gave my wife about twice as much sugar as either of them kept for themselves. My wife was profoundly moved by this generous action.

I was often called to serve as Justice of Peace without fees. As for instance, Creeping Bear had decided to take his oldest girl to Darlington and put her in school, but Mrs. Creeping Bear did not want her to go. She was in a terrible state of agitation over it.

When Creeping Bear got ready to start she took an axe in her hand and stood between him and her daughter. "If you try to take my child away I will kill you," she said in desperation.

Creeping Bear being alarmed came up to see me and said his wife opposed his taking the girl away to school, but that he was determined to do so. "I don't want any fuss with my wife, I wish you would go down and make her behave herself and let the girl go."

I found Mrs. Creeping Bear with an axe still in her hand, her eyes red with weeping.

"Go and sit down and put up your axe," I said sternly. Turning to the daughter I added: "Go with your father."

As soon as I said this Mrs. Creeping Bear began to cry. Her heart was broken. The daughter got into the wagon and Creeping Bear drove away.

This affair caused no revolt in Creeping Bear's family. When he came back his wife welcomed him with a smile, and helped him unharness his team and put it away, and the next time she came to our house she was as pleasant as ever.

During this time when my family was living among the Indians I was frequently gone from Monday morning until Saturday night and would sometimes come home in the middle of the night. My family were entirely (as some might think) at the mercy of the Indians. In reality they were under their protection. My wife felt as safe as if she were in any village or town of white people.

During the summer time we hung hammocks up under the trees and slept in them without the slightest fear, although my wife would often be awakened by a strange voice and look up and see an Indian sitting on his horse a few feet away from where she was lying. It would prove to be an Indian policeman sent out with a dispatch from the agent at Darlington or some messenger from another camp who preferred to make his ride at night rather than in the hot summer sun.

On one occasion a party of armed Kiowas came along. I was away from home, but when they started to ride up to the house my Indian friend Charcoal said, "Hold on, don't go near that house. There is no one there but a woman and some children."

One of them said: "That is all right; they will be afraid of us and will give us something to eat for the asking."

"That is the reason I do not want you to go. You are strange, and the woman and children might be afraid of you. You must not go there," and the Kiowas obeyed him.

Frequently my children would be playing around in the grove with their Indian playmates while the newspapers were full of scare-heads about imaginary Indian uprisings.

Chapter X

TROUBLE NEAR
CLOUD CHIEF

IN SEPTEMBER 1893, two years after the Cheyenne and Arapahoe country was opened for settlement, the county officers at Cloud Chief, the county seat of Washita County, were mostly Texas men, and it was popular with them to be antagonistic towards the Indians.

Texas had suffered a great deal from Indian raids and all Texas people had been taught to despise the Indians and look on them as persons to be got out of the way.

There was a Deputy Sheriff who had hopes of becoming Sheriff of the county who wished to work up some popularity to assist him in getting the office. As he had heard some complaint from the settlers in regard to the Indians carrying weapons, he thought the proper thing to do would be to arrest an Indian for carrying a gun.

The Deputy Sheriff was out to serve some papers on some cattle men, who it was claimed, had cattle in the country contrary to the quarantine laws. By the time the Sheriff reached the cattle they were crossing on the allotment of Big Smoke.

Big Smoke's camp was nearby, but as it was ration day most of the Indians had come to the headquarters for their rations, and there were only eight young men with Big Smoke left at the camp. Big Smoke was out looking for his horse and he had his gun on his saddle, as he usually carried it in order that he might kill any game that came in his way while he was hunting for his horse.

Seeing the cattle nearby he rode up to where they were. When he did so the Sheriff ordered him to give up his gun, which he did, and jumping onto his horse, ran for camp.

He told the other Indians when he ran away the Sheriff ordered him to stop, cussing him, telling him he would shoot him unless he stopped.

Big Smoke did not know that the man who had taken his gun was an officer. He supposed he was one of the cowboys who had charge of the cattle, and as he had left his gun with him the Indians resolved that they would go and get the gun. They got their ponies as soon as possible and as fast as they procured them they jumped onto their backs and rode to where the cattle were.

What took place after they reached there is told in the following letter written to me by J. D. Ballard, probate judge of Washita County. This was the white man's side of the story.

"Yesterday afternoon Mr. M——, our acting under sheriff, went up to the vicinity of the Cheyenne camp on the Washita to take charge of some cattle which had entered the county in defiance of the quarantine regulations. After placing the parties in charge under arrest, he arrested an Indian, who happened along, on a charge of carrying weapons in violation of the law. The Indian resisted and finally broke away leaving his gun in the officer's possession. In a short time twenty or thirty braves hove in view armed to the teeth, surrounded and seized the officer and disarmed him, taking his papers and everything else he had upon him. They then demanded a beef and the owner of the herd was compelled to give them one which they proceeded to slaughter, afterward returning to the cow men and the officers gun and effects. The officer bears signs of pretty rough handling, and I have no doubt that serious trouble was only averted by the absence of help on the sheriff's part.

"Now these Indians must pay the penalty of their rashness, and while I foresee the consequence of precipitate action and shall counsel prudence, I trust we can look to you for their peaceable submission to our territorial laws. Seven or eight of them can be positively identified, and I would suggest that at least that number come in and enter a plea of guilty to the charge of resisting an officer in the discharge of his duty, which constitutes a misdemeanor, punishable by a fine of $1.00 to $1000.00.

"No action will be taken until I can hear from you or until the settlers can organize for protection in case warrants shall have to be served upon the offenders."

After reading the letter I wrote to Judge Ballard not to take any action until he heard from me again; that I would send for the Indians and hear their side of the story, and I would guarantee that the guilty parties would be brought to Cloud Chief to stand a trial for any crime that they might have committed.

I sent a policeman to Big Smoke's camp with instructions to have every one who was implicated in this affair to report at my office.

In a very short time after I sent the policeman, eight Indians including Big Smoke came to my office. The story they told was as follows:

Big Smoke said, that seeing the cattle on his land he thought he would go up to where they were and see what they were doing. As he rode up to them, a man who he supposed was one of the cowboys reached out as if he wanted his gun and he handed it to him.

He said, "I thought perhaps he wanted to buy it and I might be able to trade it for a beef."

As the man took charge of the gun and did not seem to be looking at it, I reached out to take it back. When I did so he threw a cartridge into the gun and pointed it at me. I thought then the man was drunk or crazy. So I jumped onto my horse and ran away.

"He began to swear at me and as I rode away I expected to feel a bullet going through me at any time.

"I rode to camp and told the men what had happened and each one jumped onto his pony and went back as fast as he could.

"Buffalo Chips, who talked some English, was the first one to get to where the man was. He had got onto his horse and had Big Smoke's gun in the scabbard and his own across the pommel of his saddle at full cock.

"Buffalo Chips said, 'Where is Big Smoke's gun?'

"He said, 'It is on the other side of my horse in my scabbard.'

"Buffalo Chips rode around to that side where the gun was.

"While he did this the Sheriff got off his horse onto the ground.

"Just as he did so Howling Water came up behind the Sheriff and he threw his arms around the Sheriff, holding them close to his sides. Matches came up in front and grabbed hold of the Sheriff's gun and the Sheriff, thinking the Indians were going to take the gun from him and probably kill him, fought desperately. In jerking the gun around it hit the Sheriff's head and made quite a gash in his forehead. His papers flew out of his pocket and fell on the ground and the Indians succeeded in wrenching the gun from him.

"They took the cartridges—which were seven—out of the gun and then handed the empty gun to the two cowboys who stood near."

Big Smoke said he supposed the Sheriff was one of the cowboys and as the other cowboys had remained quiet and had taken no part in the affray they supposed that this particular cowboy was a kind of a crazy person, so they disarmed him.

After getting Big Smoke's gun the Indians by this time were excited, and as the Sheriff was disarmed and preparing to go home to Cloud Chief, the cowboys pointed out a beef which they told the Indians they could have, and Big Smoke feeling that himself and the other Indians had been imposed upon supposed the beef was given them to square accounts. So they went and killed a beef and took it to camp.

After learning these facts from Big Smoke I wrote his account of the affair to the probate judge and told him I believed Big Smoke's story was true, as I knew that those eight men were all that were in camp and there were only two guns in the whole camp and one of them was in the hands of the Sheriff at the time this occurred.

I told him that the Sheriff had violated the law when he disarmed Big Smoke while hunting on his own premises and he had again violated the law when he pointed the weapon at Big Smoke and threatened to shoot him. But if the Sheriff would drop the matter the Indians would do so. But if the Sheriff wanted these Indians to appear at Cloud Chief to answer for what they did, I would see that they did so without any papers being served upon them or without their being put under arrest.

The matter was let rest for some time but finally when there was a small money payment made to the Indians at the school by Major Ashley, the Indian agent, the Sheriff took action. Just as the payment was over and the Indians were preparing to go to their homes with their families, a Deputy Marshal and Deputy Sheriff appeared at school with a warrant for the eight Indians, whose names I had to give as the ones who had taken the gun from the Sheriff. They said they wanted to arrest them and take them to Cloud Chief to answer the charge of resisting an officer.

I told them the Indians were just going to their homes and there evidently was a norther coming up and they were anxious to get home before the storm broke upon them. Any time he would state when he would want these men to appear for trial I would guarantee that the Indians would be on hand.

He said no, they had come for these Indians and they intended to take them dead or alive.

I told them in this case they would have to take them without my help and I was sure there would be some lives lost before they did so, and those would not all be Indians.

On the other hand I told him if he would go back home I would see that the Indians were at Cloud Chief to answer any charge against them by the next day at 10 o'clock.

He finally agreed to this.

I notified the Indians what terms I had made and they said they would be there on time. The next morning I went to Cloud Chief and before I had got there the Indians were there. A lawyer had already got a hold of Big Smoke and had him scared up by telling him he would surely go to jail if he did not employ the lawyer to defend him. Big Smoke had promised him a pony if he would defend him in the case.

When I got there the Indians were considerably excited as lawyers had been after them all trying to get to be their attorneys. Big Smoke came up to me very much excited and said, "I want you to push hard for me as I do not want to go to jail; I have already given this man a horse to help me in my case."

I told Big Smoke not to give any horse. I would see that he did not go to jail. I then went before the judge and the case was called. I waived examination in behalf of the Indians and gave bond for their appearance at the next court. Then I turned around and had the Deputy Sheriff arrested under two charges—one for having taken the gun from the Indian contrary to law while the Indian was hunting on his own ground; the other for pointing the gun at the Indian and threatening to kill him.

The Deputy Sheriff also waived examination and gave

bond to appear for trial at the next term of court.

The matter was never carried any further on the part of the Deputy Sheriff. The case was brought up supposing the Indians had money after this payment and probably in hopes they could scare them out of quite a portion of it.

This will show some of the discouraging conditions of the Indian situation at the first settlement of their lands by white men. On the other hand there were a great many good citizens who were willing to be helpful to the Indians and whom the Indians learned to respect and have confidence in.

Appendix

TRADITION OF

THE CHEYENNE INDIANS

EDITOR'S NOTE—The interesting account which follows was published by Mr. Seger in a pamphlet issued by the Arapahoe *Bee*. It is reproduced faithfully, except for a number of illustrations which accompanied the original.

❋   ❋   ❋

John H. Seger—The only white man ever intrusted with the Tradition of the Cheyenne Indians, came to Darlington in 1872. Darlington was then the Cheyenne & Arapaho Indian Agency. He was in charge of the Indian School at Darlington for five years, which included the Cheyenne School, the Arapaho School and a school for 40 children of the Northern Cheyenne, when they were moved down to Darlington after the battle in which General Custer was killed. He moved the Cheyennes & Arapahoes, an affiliated tribe, to what was afterwards called Seger Colony. There he built up the Seger School and was in charge of it for 12 years.

SEGER INDIAN SCHOOL, COLONY, OKLAHOMA, 1900

Left to right: Hospital, Teachers' Building, Water-tower,
School and Dormitory Building.

Preface

The tradition of the Cheyennes as told to John H. Seger, by one who was appointed to keep this tradition.

Preface of the relation of the story giving the tradition of the Cheyennes.

This story is the history of the tribe of Cheyenne Indians and it is their history as far back as they know anything of their history and it has been handed down by word of mouth from generation to generation, and John H. Seger fully believes that he is the only white man who knows this tradition and he now publishes it that it may be preserved, also that the Cheyennes may have a record of their origin.

It was the spring of the year when John H. Seger had charge of the Cheyenne and Arapaho Indians, at what is known as Seger Colony, that a prominent Cheyenne Chief came to him and said: "when is the best time to plant corn?" Seger replied, "plant corn when the oak leaves are the size of a squirrel's foot and plant potatoes when the elm buds begin to swell and plant corn when the moon is light because it grows above ground and plant potatoes when the moon is dark because thy grow below ground. I suppose when the white man first came to this country that he found the Indians raising corn and potatoes, and when the white man asked the Indians when was the best time to plant them the Indian told him as I told you which was to plant corn when the oak leaves were the size of a squirrel's foot."

The Indian replied, "I suppose that is so, for the Cheyennes planted corn before they hunted buffalo. I have a good mind to tell you about it."

131

Seger said, "is that so, tell me all about it, for I thought the Indians always hunted buffalo."

The Indian says, "I will do so if you will write it down and some day have it printed in a book and will not give the name of the one who told it to you. The reason I ask this is because it is our history and I am of those who are appointed to keep it, each one is required to make a vow and promise to the Great Spirit that he will never tell it as a story and will not tell it except in the presence of two others who are appointed to tell it and they must agree to every word as it is told, before the one who is telling it can go on. And should I tell this history to you I would be breaking my vow and promise, and would be censured because of it, and the reason why I would tell it to you is because the habits and customs of the Cheyennes are changing and we are not repeating this history as often as we did in the past and we are not adding of late any new history and I can see that as the Cheyennes take up the white people's ways and customs, more and more we will let our old customs disappear and to preserve our history is the only thing that would induce me to violate my vow by telling this history to you. So if you will promise me faithfully to write it down and have it printed that our children and their children can know the past history of their tribe, I will give it to you." I promised.

So this booklet is the fulfillment of my promise to him.

Tradition of the Cheyenne Indians

The tradition of the Cheyennes as told to John H. Seger in the year of 1905, by one who was appointed to keep the tradition. This story is considered sacred and is no falsehood.

A long time ago before the Cheyennes ever heard of or saw a white man the Cheyennes lived in the north, in a much colder country than this where we live now. We were a large and hearty people in those days.

Although it was a cold climate the men, women and children went naked, and wore no clothing. In very cold weather we would crawl into caves or hollow logs and would carry dry leaves and make nests or beds with them and we would pile up very much like some animals will do to keep warm and we would remain that way during a snow storm.

We would walk across the rivers and streams on the ice in our bare feet and thought nothing of it,—the same as a bear or panther could do.

We had no way of getting food but such as we could get or kill with our hands. We could climb trees and get young squirrels or panthers or any kind of animals that were young and helpless or we could get young birds from the nests or could get bird's eggs. We run in herds like a herd of buffalo or antelope. We had no families and the mother only cared for her children when they were young and helpless very much the same as a cow cares for her calf.

As our tribe increased food became difficult to get. The first help we had in getting a living was brought about in this way: A Cheyenne woman lost a small child that was nursing. Soon after her child died she had found a nest of young kitten panthers, she waited until the mother panther was away to hunt food, then she went and took one of the young panthers out of the nest and ran off with it and the young panther gave a moan or whine which sounded like the cry of the baby she had lost and the reminder of her dead babe caused the woman to hug the kitten panther to her breast and when she did so the kitten panther which no doubt was hungry began nursing the woman. Thus it was taking the place of her dead babe and an affection for the kitten panther sprang into her heart and the woman loved this kitten panther and she raised it as if it had been her own child, and as it grew up it would kill deer and other large game and furnished food for the Cheyennes much easier than they could get it in any other way.

So other women got hold of young panthers and raised them the same way as this woman had done. And they not only got by the help of these panthers their food much easier than they had done previously to their getting the panther, but they had to take the hide off the deer and other game they got by the help of the panther. This made it necessary for them to get something to cut the hides with so they got pieces of flint stone that had sharp edges, which enabled them to cut the hides off of the animals the panthers killed. They found these hides would keep them warmer than leaves when laid over them, so they used them in this way.

There was another tribe of Indians that used to fight with them and attack them when they crossed each others paths. This tribe would steal the children of the Cheyennes and their women also, and keep possession of them. The Cheyennes were not so warlike as this other tribe, yet the other tribe was afraid to meet the Cheyennes openly, because the Cheyennes were so large and strong. So the other tribe would come at night and come on to them stealthily and bear away their women and children. So the Cheyennes went to war against this tribe that was menace to them and they killed them with clubs and stones.

After the Cheyennes had killed many of this tribe and captured many of them as prisoners they were not bothered by them. Since the Cheyennes began to use the hides of animals, which the panthers had killed they not only used the hides to cover over them in cold weather but some times they would use them to tie around themselves to protect their bodies from the cold, thus they could go about in the cold much better than they could before they got these hides and they would use the hides to construct rude shelters from the cold.

A change came in the lives of the Cheyennes, which was brought about by a great flood of water which covered the earth where the Cheyennes were then living. We don't know just where it was but we think it was in the valley of the Missouri river up near its head. It seems we were in a valley where there were mountains on the side of the valley. What was the cause of the flood we do not know, whether it was an earthquake or a cloud burst, but very suddenly the earth was covered with swimming water and everyone had to take care of himself and the only way they could do this was to swim toward the mountains which were far away. There were but few who escaped drowning and when they did so they landed alone. Their panthers were all drowned. Thus they were when they reached land. Alone and with nothing but their hands to provide their food. They were naked and on a mountainous barren land and at first only one in a place. It was hard work to get any thing to live on, yet they remembered the help the panthers had given them and the use they had made of the hides of the game the panthers had killed and how they had made use of the sharp flint stones to skin their game.

The remembrance of this seemed to inspire them to use their minds to study ways of getting food, so they used their minds to study out ways to get food. There was no game in these mountains like there was in the valley and lower land where they lived before the flood.

There were small trees. They used sharp flint stone to scrape off the bark which they ate to keep from starving. There were fish in the mountain brooks, they studied up ways of getting them which was principally by trapping them, which was done by putting something in the brook where there was but little water, then drive the fish to the place where they could catch them with their hands or hit them with a club or stone.

Sometimes when a Cheyenne reached the land when swimming out of the flood, it was a long time before he would meet another one of the tribe who had like himself escaped. When he did so, this was the first time that love sprang up in their hearts one for another. After the flood when two would meet after wandering around alone for we know not how long, it might have been for months or years, at the sight of each other love seemed to spring into their hearts and they would run to meet with outspread arms and would clasp each other to their bosoms in a loving embrace. This love which was kindled at the sight of each other did not die, but caused them to form families. If one was a man and the other a woman, they afterwards lived together as man and wife and when children were born they loved them even after they were grown up. As the numbers of those who had escaped the flood become greater, as they drifted together and children were born it was necessary for them to invent other means to get food which they did. They used clubs to kill game with that they could not get with their hands. Their experience in the flood caused them to be afraid to again go into the valley where they lived when the floods came, so they necessarily had to exert themselves to get food to live on, to do this they became very skillful in handling the club, they learned to throw a club to kill game they could not reach otherwise.

At the time of the flood there was one band of Cheyennes that disappeared and those who escaped never have been heard of nor saw one of them since the flood. Yet even to this day if they meet a member of a tribe of Indians they have never met before they at once begin an inquiry to find out whether they might be the part of the tribe that was lost in the flood, yet they have never found any of them.

The Cheyennes kept increasing in numbers and had to spread out over a greater area of territory until they met another tribe of Indians who spoke a different language, yet was living like they themselves were, and were also using clubs for weapons. With the two tribes being so near together, game became scarce and the tribe they met regarded the Cheyennes as intruders on their hunting grounds, so made an attack on them, as the tribes they met were numerous it was very hard for the Cheyennes to keep them from overpowering them. But about this time there was one of the Cheyennes who was very strong. It was believed that the

Great Spirit gave him strength to do things. The Great Spirit also provided him with a large club and told him that any one whom he hit with it would be killed. (This is the first time the Great Spirit is mentioned in their tradition.)

So the Cheyennes knew that wherever this man met the enemy their side would win because the Great Spirit was with him. They also had bows and arrows with points of stone. They also used stone hammers. They had no iron so they used bones and stone instead. Used flint and bones for knives. The other tribe who had been at war with the Cheyennes were soon driven out of the country.

And the Cheyennes never knew what became of them. The flood had brought much trouble. We seemed to wake up and we reasoned more. We were more kind and human. We began to make friends with other tribes when we met them. One time we had placed our camp in the shape of a horse-shoe the opened end being towards the rising sun. We were camped on a level piece of land and below our camp was a large spring, which gushed out from the foot of a bluff. In the midst of our camp were some young men playing the hoop game and some were playing the game of chance, the basket game. (This is the first time that gambling was spoken of in tradition. The basket game that they used then is used by them today).

It was at a time when game was scarce, and the Cheyennes were very hungry. There was one Indian watching the game who dressed very peculiar and different from the rest. This man had a painted hide, which he wore around him as he stood watching the game. He had a feather stuck in his hair, and it was worn different than a feather was worn by any other Indian, soon another Indian came and stood by the first, and he was dressed in the same way as the first mentioned Indian was dressed. When he saw this he said, "why are you mocking me, by dressing like me?" The 2nd one said, "that it is you that is mocking me." They were soon engaged in a quarrel, and a large crowd gathered around them. The first Indian said, "that it is you that is mocking me, for I was told to dress this way by a person in that spring." "So was I," the other Indian said, "if you are telling the truth follow me into the spring, and if you can go into the spring like I can, then I will know that you are not telling a lie." So the Indian dove headfirst into the spring. The other Indian followed him, they came out together where an old woman was baking bread made of corn. The woman asked them why they come there together, and she had one sit on the right of her and the other on the left, then asked them what they came there for? They said that their people were very near starving, and they were told by the Great Spirit, to come there and they would find an old woman who would tell them what to do. She said, "I know all about it and that is the reason I have prepared something for your people to eat." The old woman then showed them a field of corn, which extended as far as they could see. Then she showed them a large herd of buffalo which extended as far as they could see. The old woman said she knew that they needed food and the Great Spirit had heard their prayers and had instructed her to prepare food for them. The old woman taught them how to plant corn and told them how to kill buffalo and she gave the two men buffalo meat and corn bread to eat, and told them that the Great Spirit would give them food to live on instead of the small animals that they had been living on, for as their people were more numerous they would need more to live on than in the past. She then showed them how to make corn into bread and told them how to dress the buffalo. When the old woman had given them the necessary instructions they were ready to go out of the spring. She gave them corn bread and buffalo meat to feed their people and corn to plant. She told them to feed their people with the corn bread and meat which she gave them. She told them to begin and feed the men first as they would have to hunt the game and provide the meat for the people to eat. When they were fed and satisfied, she said, "that they should feed the women for they were to cook the food and care for the camp and last they were to feed the children and orphans and those who were dependent and after they were all satisfied there would be nothing left of the food she gave.

She told them when they went out the buffalo would follow them. The men went out and they fed the people like they were instructed to do and the people were all satisfied. After they were through eating every one was instructed to go into their tepees so that not to frighten buffalo when they came out of the spring. One buffalo came out, he looked around then kicked up his heels and went back into the spring, then three buffalo cows came out and looked around, they then went back into the spring. Then a noise like thunder was heard and soon a herd of buffalo came pouring out of a spring, they kept coming out until they filled the valley below the spring with buffalo, and they went to grazing. Then one of them who came out of the spring showed them how to kill the buffalo and dress it. The other man taught them how to plant the corn and tend it, thus the buffalo and the corn gave the Indians plenty of food. After they had planted and tended their corn they lived on it through the winter, while the buffalo had drifted south to spend the winter.

The Cheyennes had no way to carry their bedding and camp equipage, as they now had begun to use the buffalo robes to cover their tepees and also for bedding. They could not take this with them and follow the buffalo very far south. During the time that had passed by the Cheyennes had met up with other tribes, who disputed with them the right to the hunting ground. Other tribes who opposed them, would steal into their camp at night when they were sleeping and attack them. To prevent this the Cheyennes captured young wolves or wild dogs and raised them as pets and they would guard their camps at night and now since they were killing buffalo they could provide plenty of meat for these dogs and they soon had a large number of them in camp. They began to pack their camp equipage on these dogs when they followed the buffalo on their way south in the fall and with the help of the dogs they were enabled to follow the buffalo much farther than they could do before they had the dogs to carry their camp equipage, but all had to go on foot and the women carried the young children on their backs. The Cheyenne women were very strong in those days, they would give birth to a child and the next day would take the child and keep up with the tribe. In the fall as they could not carry corn with them, they would store it away in caves, so they would have it when they came back from following the buffalo.

Some other tribe came to their hunting ground when they were gone, and found their corn which they had stored away in a cave. They took a part of it so when the Cheyennes came

141

back from following the buffalo, they were short of something to eat. Yet as the Indians had not taken all their corn, they had corn to plant but finally some white men came up a stream in a boat. They were the first white men they had ever seen or heard of. They did not molest the white men and they soon went down the stream again and afterwards the white men came up the stream to their hunting grounds. While the Cheyennes were away after buffalo and the white men found the Cheyennes' corn which they had stored away and the white men took all the corn they had left and carried it off and did not leave any for seed. When the Cheyennes came back and found the corn was gone there was no other way for them to do but to turn back and follow the buffalo south. This was very hard for them to do as they had nothing but dogs to carry their food and camp equipage. As the men did the hunting the women had to move the camp. They were obliged to move so slow that when a cold spell of weather came and the buffalo moved faster toward the south and traveled a long ways before they settled down to graze. The Cheyennes were unable to keep up with them and had it not been for the large number of dogs they had with them of which they killed and ate, they would have starved to death before they could catch up with the buffalo again. They went much further south than ever before and did not go as far north as their old hunting ground.

On one of their trips south they met some Mexicans who were riding ponies, these were the first ponies they had ever seen. One day they came across a pony and they caught him and he proved to be gentle and they packed him and as he could carry much more than many dogs they sent a party

142

down into Mexico and brought back a herd of ponies with them. They soon learned to use these ponies and it enabled them to get their living much easier and it changed their way of living to a great extent.

The pony very soon became the standard of value. As time went on they came in contact with the white man, since which time their Indian customs have been changing and as one old Indian man said, "tribes of people are like the waves of the ocean which roll along until it strikes the shore then it vanishes, but another wave takes its place and follows it until it too strikes the shore, when it also vanishes, so it will be with tribes of people, one tribe follows another, when one tribe passes away, another takes its place, and it will be so until eternity."

FOOT NOTE—*This is the full and complete tradition of the Cheyenne Indians. A history kept by word of mouth you will understand is necessarily short and brief. It is printed to preserve it for the Indians and to keep my promise to the Indians.*

JOHN H. SEGER.

The Civilization of the American Indian Series

of which *Early Days Among the Cheyenne and Arapahoe Indians* was the fifth volume, was inaugurated in 1932 by the University of Oklahoma Press, and has as its purpose the reconstruction of American Indian civilization by presenting aboriginal, historical, and contemporary Indian life. The following list is complete as of the date of the reissuing of this volume:

1. Alfred Barnaby Thomas. *Forgotten Frontiers*: A Study of the Spanish Indian Policy of Don Juan Bautista de Anza, Governor of New Mexico, 1777–1787. Out of print.
2. Grant Foreman. *Indian Removal*: The Emigration of the Five Civilized Tribes of Indians.
3. John Joseph Mathews, *Wah'Kon-Tah*: The Osage and the White Man's Road. Out of print.
4. Grant Foreman. *Advancing the Frontier, 1830–1860*. Out of print.
5. John Homer Seger. *Early Days Among the Cheyenne and Arapahoe Indians*. Edited by Stanley Vestal.
6. Angie Debo. *The Rise and Fall of the Choctaw Republic*. Out of print.
7. Stanley Vestal. *New Sources of Indian History, 1850–1891*. Out of print.
8. Grant Foreman. *The Five Civilized Tribes*.
9. Alfred Barnaby Thomas. *After Coronado*: Spanish Exploration Northeast of New Mexico, 1696–1727. Out of print.
10. Frank G. Speck. *Naskapi*: The Savage Hunters of the Labrador Peninsula.
11. Elaine Goodale Eastman. *Pratt*: *The Red Man's Moses*.
12. Althea Bass. *Cherokee Messenger*: A Life of Samuel Austin Worcester.
13. Thomas Wildcat Alford. *Civilization*. As told to Florence Drake.
14. Grant Foreman. *Indians and Pioneers*: The Story of the American Southwest Before 1830.
15. George E. Hyde. *Red Cloud's Folk*: A History of the Oglala Sioux Indians. Out of print.

144

16. Grant Foreman. *Sequoyah*. Out of print.
17. Morris L. Wardell. *A Political History of the Cherokee Nation, 1838–1907*.
18. John Walton Caughey. *McGillivray of the Creeks*. Out of print.
19. Edward Everett Dale and Gaston Litton. *Cherokee Cavaliers*: Forty Years of Cherokee History as Told in the Correspondence of the Ridge-Watie-Boudinot Family. Out of print.
20. Ralph Henry Gabriel. *Elias Boudinot, Cherokee, and His America*.
21. Karl N. Llewellyn and E. Adamson Hoebel. *The Cheyenne Way*: Conflict and Case Law in Primitive Jurisprudence.
22. Angie Debo. *The Road to Disappearance*.
23. Oliver La Farge and others. *The Changing Indian*. Out of print.
24. Carolyn Thomas Foreman. *Indians Abroad*. Out of print.
25. John Adair. *The Navajo and Pueblo Silversmiths*.
26. Alice Marriott. *The Ten Grandmothers*.
27. Alice Marriott. *María*: The Potter of San Ildefonso.
28. Edward Everett Dale. *The Indians of the Southwest*: A Century of Development Under the United States.
29. Adrián Recinos. *Popol Vuh*: The Sacred Book of the Ancient Quiché Maya. English version by Delia Goetz and Sylvanus G. Morley from the translation of Adrián Recinos.
30. Walter Collins O'Kane. *Sun in the Sky*.
31. Stanley A. Stubbs. *Bird's-Eye View of the Pueblos*.
32. Katharine C. Turner. *Red Men Calling on the Great White Father*.
33. Muriel H. Wright. *A Guide to the Indian Tribes of Oklahoma*.
34. Ernest Wallace and E. Adamson Hoebel. *The Comanches*: Lords of the South Plains.
35. Walter Collins O'Kane. *The Hopis*: Portrait of a Desert People.
36. Joseph Epes Brown. *The Sacred Pipe*: Black Elk's Account of the Seven Rites of the Oglala Sioux.
37. Adrián Recinos and Delia Goetz. *The Annals of the Cakchiquels*. Translated from the Cakchiquel Maya, with *Title of the Lords of Totonicapán*, translated from the Quiché text into Spanish by Dionisio José Chonay, English version by Delia Goetz.

145

38. R. S. Cotterill. *The Southern Indians*: The Story of the Civilized Tribes Before Removal.
39. J. Eric S. Thompson. *The Rise and Fall of Maya Civilization.*
40. Robert Emmitt. *The Last War Trail*: The Utes and the Settlement of Colorado.
41. Frank Gilbert Roe. *The Indian and the Horse.*
42. Francis Haines. *The Nez Percés*: Tribesmen of the Columbia Plateau.
43. Ruth M. Underhill. *The Navajos.*
44. George Bird Grinnell. *The Fighting Cheyennes.*

Early Days

among the Cheyenne and Arapahoe Indians

The text of this book has been set on the Linotype in William Addison Dwiggins's *Caledonia*, derived from, but improving upon, the type style known as Scotch Roman. It is used in the eleven-point size, with three points of leading.

Accompanying the *Caledonia* as a display face on title page and chapter heads is Rudolf Koch's rugged *Neuland*, one of the few contemporary types for which punches were cut by hand. It is set by hand, as is customary with most display types. The wide use of display types—that is, types that contrast in style or weight with body or text types came in the present century, probably as a result of the renaissance of lettering which followed the influence of Edward Johnston of England and Rudolf von Larisch of Austria.

A freely drawn version of a decoration by a plains Indian, taken from an old parfleche, adorns the title page.